180 Days of Printing
Beginning

Publishing Credits

Corinne Burton, M.A.Ed., *Publisher*
Emily R. Smith, M.A.Ed., *Senior VP of Content Development*
Véronique Bos, *Vice President of Creative*
Andrew Greene, M.A.Ed., *Senior Content Manager*
Jill Malcolm, *Graphic Designer*

Standards

© Copyright 2007–2021 Texas Education Agency (TEA). All Rights Reserved.
© 2012 English–Language Arts Content Standards for California Public Schools by the California Department of Education.
© Copyright 2010 National Governors Association Center for Best Practices and Council of Chief State School Officers. All rights reserved.

Image Credits: all images from iStock and/or Shutterstock

A division of Teacher Created Materials
5482 Argosy Avenue
Huntington Beach, CA 92649
www.tcmpub.com/shell-education
ISBN 978-1-0876-6241-1
© 2023 Shell Educational Publishing, Inc.
Printed in USA. WOR004

Table of Contents

Introduction

Weekly Practice Pages

Table of Contents *(cont.)*

Weekly Practice Pages

Appendix

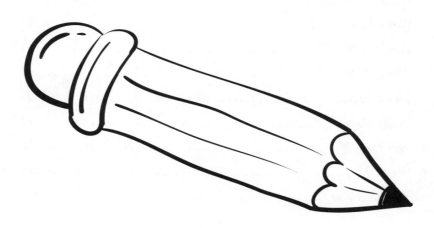

Foundations for Handwriting

Welcome to *180 Days of Handwriting: Beginning*! Students will learn the foundations for handwriting and practice letter formation basics in this book. These practice pages provide fun and engaging ways for young learners to develop good handwriting habits.

Hand-eye Coordination

Hand-eye coordination is essential for handwriting. Students track lines with their eyes to guide, direct, and control hand movement. Coordination allows students to write on the line, properly space letters, write proper letter size, and more. This developmental approach is also seen in research-based programs, such as Handwriting Without Tears. Hand-eye coordination is reinforced throughout this book through engaging, age-appropriate activities and practice pages.

Shapes

Drawing shapes provides a foundation for letter formation. As students become more familiar with strokes to write basic shapes, they become more capable of writing letters. Shapes help bridge the gap between the general strokes of drawing and the strokes that will later form letters.

Drawing

Drawing helps students develop fine-motor skills that extend to handwriting, such as holding a writing instrument correctly and applying the correct amount of force and speed to mark paper. Drawing also helps students with basic line formation. Drawing keeps young writers engaged through play-based activities and practice pages.

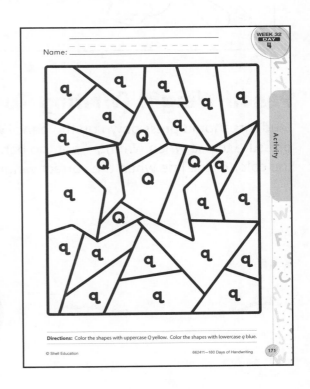

Coloring

Coloring reinforces basic stroke formation along with hand-eye coordination. As a pre-writing skill, coloring helps students develop fine-motor skills later used in letter formation. Students also become more aware of spacing, which is essential for writing words and sentences.

Getting Ready to Write

Pencil Grip

Students will naturally find their dominant hand as they learn to properly grip writing instruments. Help students decide which hand is more comfortable to write with, and guide them to alternate hands if they show no clear preference. Teach students a pencil grip with their pointer finger on the top, thumb on the side, and three fingers below the pencil to support the grip. Encourage students to use this pencil grip as they work through the pages of the book.

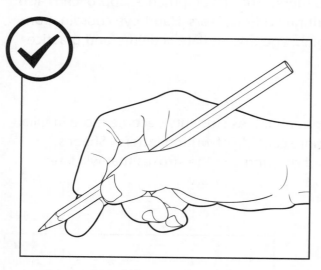
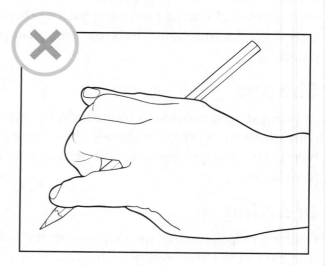

Pencil Weight (Writing Too Hard or Too Soft)

Students should press down on the pencil with medium weight. Demonstrate the proper pressure to use when writing—not too hard and not too soft. Bring students' attention to the color of the line when the correct weight is used.

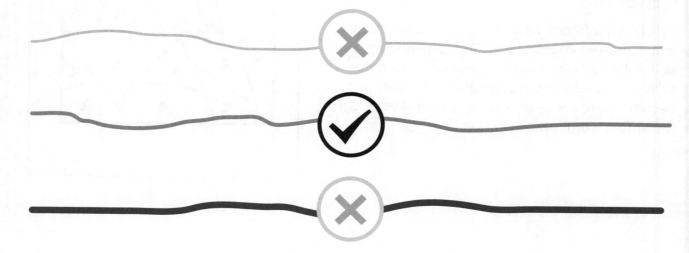

Letter Spacing

Teach students proper letter spacing within a word and between words in a sentence. Demonstrate that letters in a word do not touch but have minimal space between them. As students grasp spacing within words, demonstrate the required spacing between words. Encourage students to use their pointer fingers or popsicle sticks to properly space the words. Reinforce letter spacing as students practice writing uppercase and lowercase letters on the review pages.

Letter Reversal

Some letter reversal is natural as students learn to write, especially with *p, q, d,* and *b*. Be sure to correct students in the case that they reverse letters and encourage quality letter formation instead of quantity. Provide adequate practice time so students understand the strokes for a particular letter. Letters in this program are presented by stroke, so encourage a focus on stroke directionality and order.

Letter Presentation Order

To give students a strong foundation in handwriting, this book builds off the smallest handwriting units—strokes. By presenting letters by strokes instead of alphabetical order, students can more easily make connections on how to write them. The letter presentation order also takes high-frequency letters into account, quickly providing a foundation to begin writing words and sentences. Presenting letters by stroke also gives students ample practice time to create and refine motor control when creating letter strokes. The use of repetition in presenting strokes across multiple weeks provides the practice young learners need to increase proficiency.

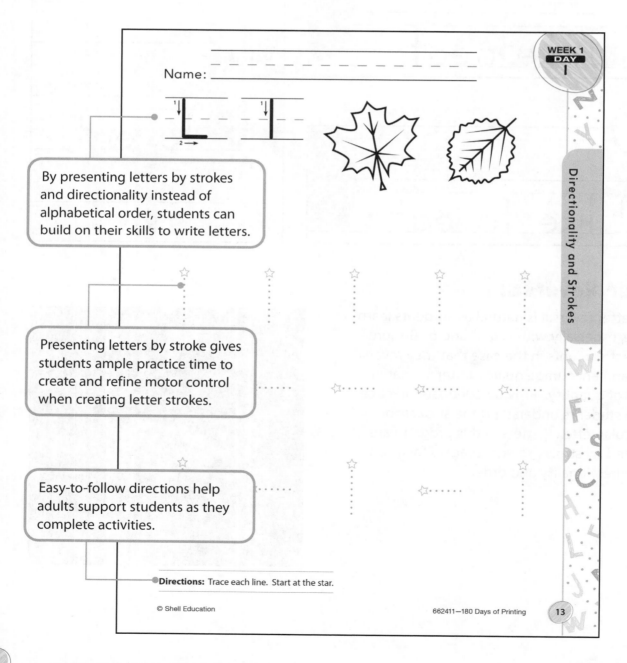

By presenting letters by strokes and directionality instead of alphabetical order, students can build on their skills to write letters.

Presenting letters by stroke gives students ample practice time to create and refine motor control when creating letter strokes.

Easy-to-follow directions help adults support students as they complete activities.

Directions: Trace each line. Start at the star.

© Shell Education   662411—180 Days of Printing   13

WEEK 1
DAY
1

Directionality and Strokes

Sight Words

This program takes a holistic approach to handwriting, teaching not only individual letters but also how they fit into words and sentences. High-frequency words pulled from Dr. Edward Fry's Instant Words list and Dr. Edward Dolch's Most Common Words list allow students to practice words they will see and write frequently. The use of these sight words to practice handwriting increases letter awareness as students are exposed to these letters and words in other age-appropriate learning materials.

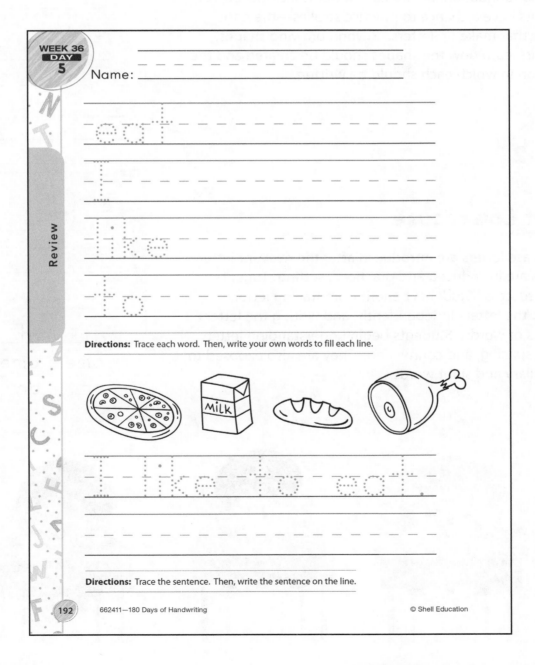

WEEK 36
DAY
5
Name:

Review

eat

I

like

to

Directions: Trace each word. Then, write your own words to fill each line.

I like to eat

Directions: Trace the sentence. Then, write the sentence on the line.

192   662411—180 Days of Handwriting   © Shell Education

How to Use This Book

Day 1

Directionality and Strokes

180 Days of Printing: Beginning prioritizes giving students a strong foundation. Before each letter is introduced, students have a chance to practice strokes—the basic shapes that make up letters. Beyond drawing shapes, students learn how the shapes should be created and the direction in which each should be written.

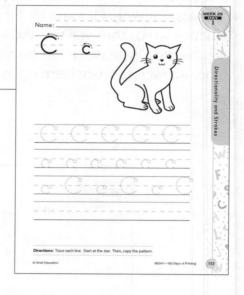

Day 2

Print Lowercase

Lowercase letters are introduced after the relevant letter strokes are introduced and practiced, setting students up for success. Students benefit from tracing letters, writing the letters independently, and writing the letters as parts of words. Students begin understanding letter shape, spacing, and connection. They are also exposed to vocabulary and sight words.

Day 3

Print Uppercase

Uppercase letters are introduced after lowercase letters, continuing to build on relevant strokes. Students benefit from tracing letters, writing letters independently, and writing letters as parts of words. Students practice letter shapes, spacing, and connections as they write proper nouns.

Day 4

Activity

Activities give students chances to practice strokes, directionality, and letter recognition in engaging ways. In this book, these activities focus on developing fine-motor skills while building on letter recognition.

Day 5

Review

A key to mastering handwriting is repetition. Weekly reviews provide students with extra practice. The reviews build on previous skills to practice letter spacing and connections and move toward more independent writing. The reviews also provide opportunities to practice sight words through repetition.

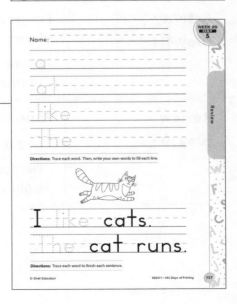

Standards Correlations

Shell Education is committed to producing educational materials that are research and standards based. To support this effort, this resource is correlated to the academic standards of all 50 states, the District of Columbia, the Department of Defense Dependent Schools, and the Canadian provinces. A correlation is also provided for key professional educational organizations.

To print a customized correlation report for your state, please visit our website at **www.tcmpub.com/administrators/correlations** and follow the online directions. If you require assistance in printing correlation reports, please contact the Customer Service Department at 1-800-858-7339.

Stroke and Directionality (Day 1)	**Foundational Skills: Adjust grasp and body position for increased control in drawing and writing.** • Demonstrate proper finger grasp. • Begin using nondominant hand to hold paper to maintain control.
Print Lowercase and Uppercase (Days 2 and 3)	**Foundational Skills: Print all upper- and lowercase letters.** • Recognize and print all upper- and lowercase letters of the alphabet. **Foundational Skills: Capitalize dates and names of people.** • Demonstrate understanding of capitalization. **Foundational Skills: Capitalize holidays, product names, and geographic names.** • Demonstrate understanding of capitalization.
Activity (Day 4)	**Foundational Skills: Practice words phonetically, drawing on phonemic awareness and spelling conventions.** • Demonstrate the ability to decode new vocabulary through phonemic and spelling awareness.
Review (Day 5)	**Foundational Skills: Use frequently occurring nouns and verbs.** • Begin reading and writing high-frequency nouns and verbs. • Demonstrate basic comprehension of nouns and verbs through sight words.

Name: _____

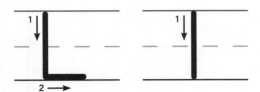

Directions: Start at the star. Trace each line.

Name: _____

Print Lowercase

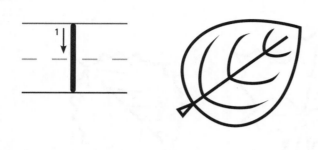

$1\downarrow$ l

Directions: Start at the star. Trace each letter. Then, write your own letters to fill the lines.

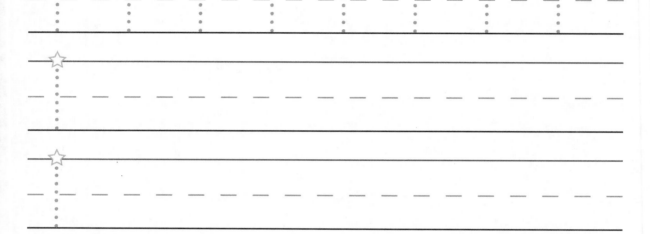

ion   ion

eaf   eaf

ock   ock

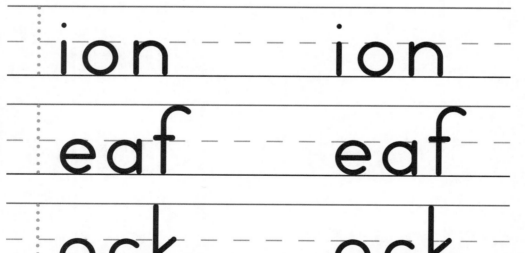

Directions: Trace the letters. Then, write the missing letter to complete each word.

Name: _____

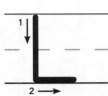

Directions: Start at the star. Trace each letter. Then, write your own letters to fill the lines.

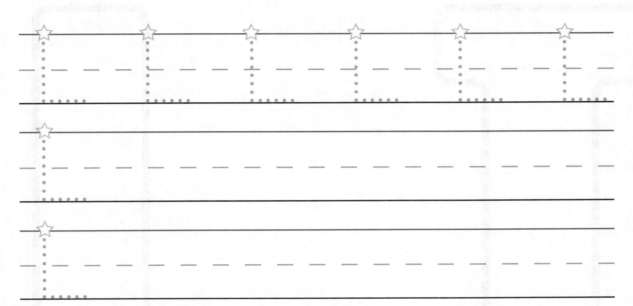

eo   eo

una   una

isa   isa

Directions: Trace the letters. Then, write the missing letter to complete each name.

Name: _____

Activity

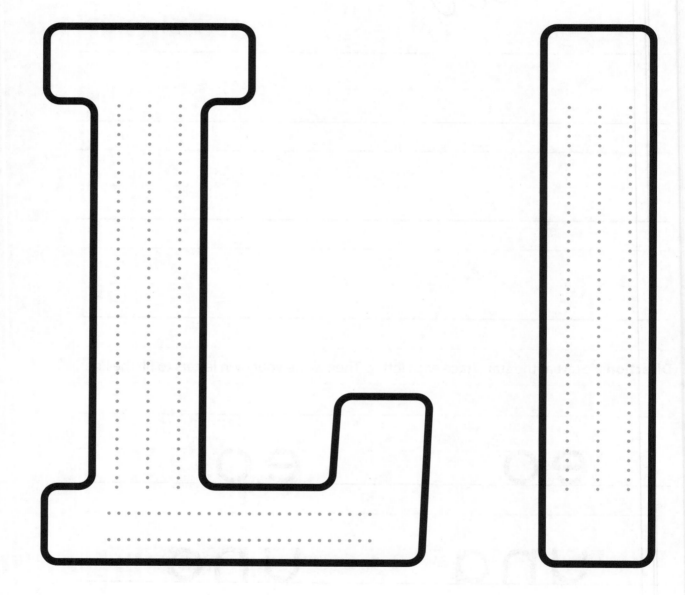

Directions: Trace each line. Then, decorate the letters.

130193—180 Days of Printing: Beginning

Name: _____

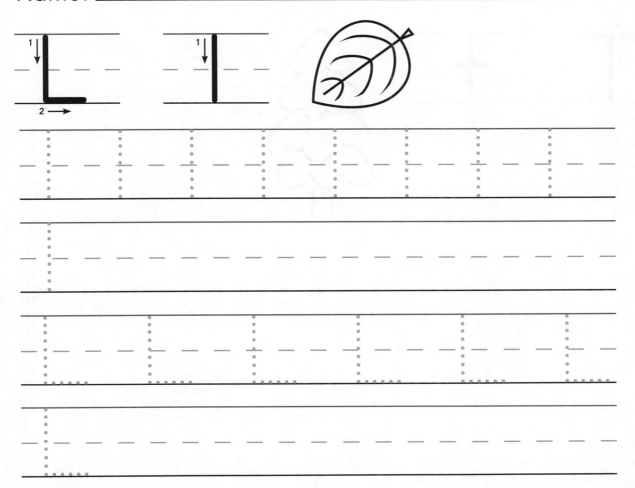

Directions: Trace the letters. Then, write your own letters to fill each line.

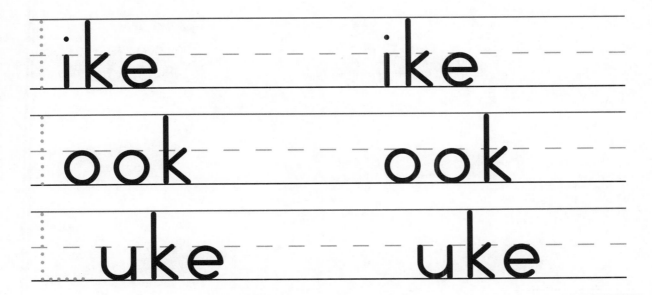

Directions: Trace the letters. Then, write the missing letter to complete each word or name.

Directionality and Strokes

Name: _____

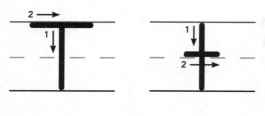

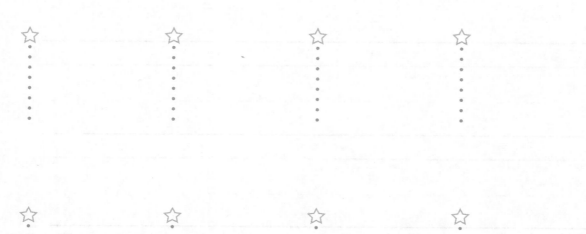

Directions: Start at the star. Trace each line.

Name: _____

Directions: Start at the star. Trace each letter. Then, write your own letters to fill the lines.

ree   ree

aco   aco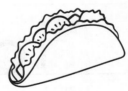

oe   oe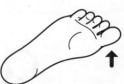

Directions: Trace the letters. Then, write the missing letter to complete each word.

Print Uppercase

Name: _____

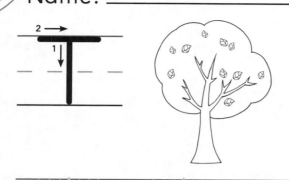

Directions: Start at the star. Trace each letter. Then, write your own letters to fill the lines.

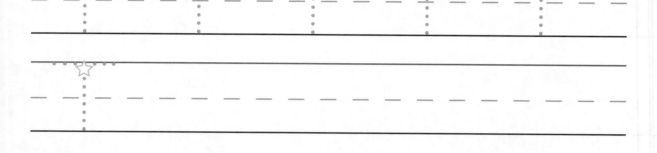

Directions: Trace the letters. Then, write the missing letter to complete each name.

Name: _____

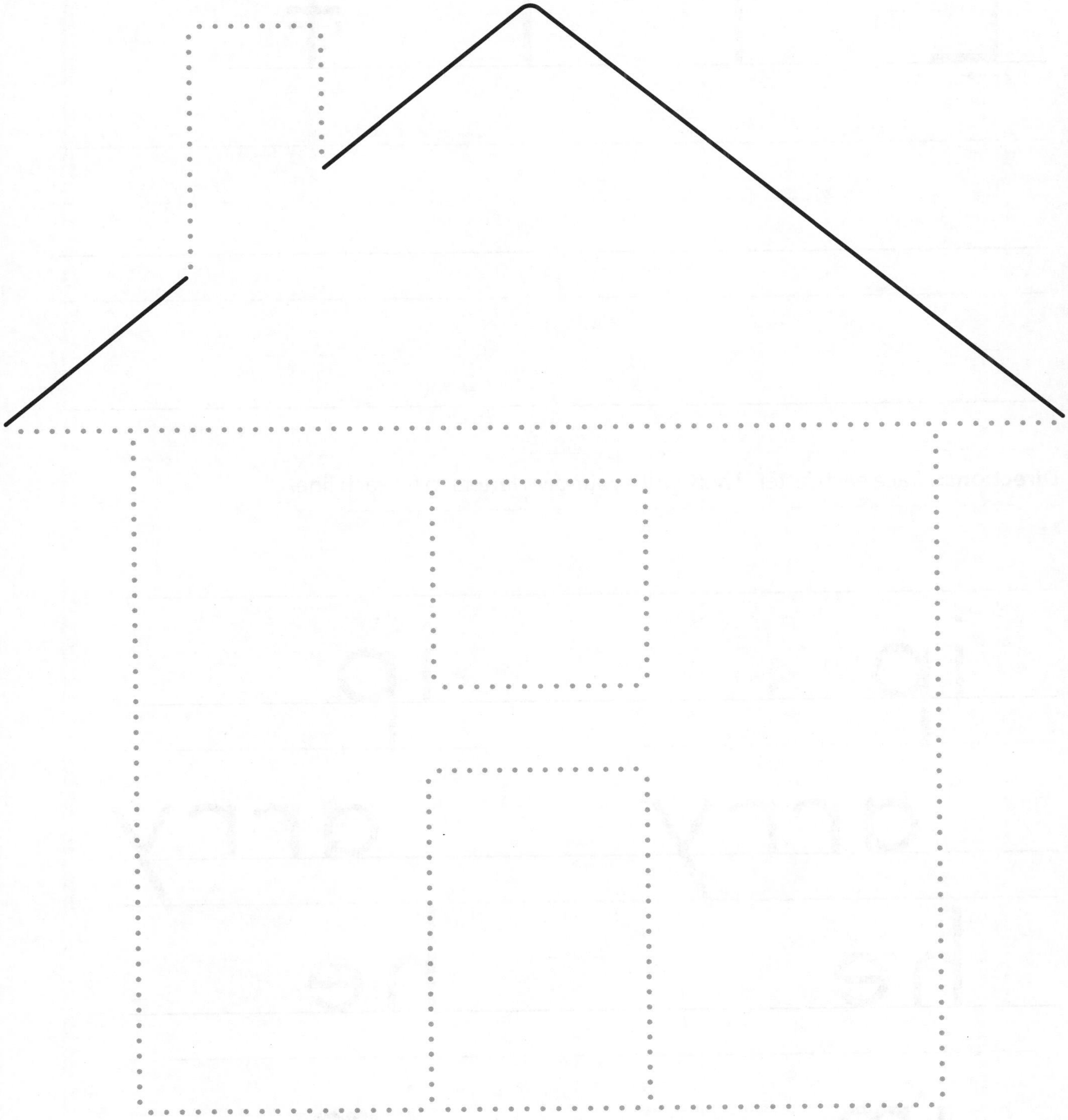

Activity

Directions: Trace each line to finish the picture. Draw your own decorations on the house.

Name: _____

Review

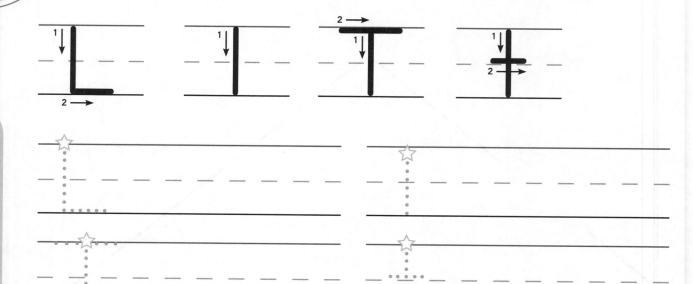

Directions: Trace each letter. Then, write your own letters to fill each line.

Directions: Trace the letters. Then, write the missing letter to complete each word or name.

Name: _____

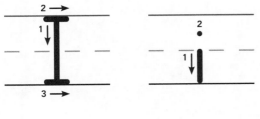

Directions: Start at the star. Trace each line.

Directions: Place a dot in each circle.

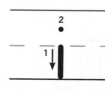

Name: _____

Print Lowercase

Directions: Start at the star. Trace each letter. Then, write your own letters to fill the lines.

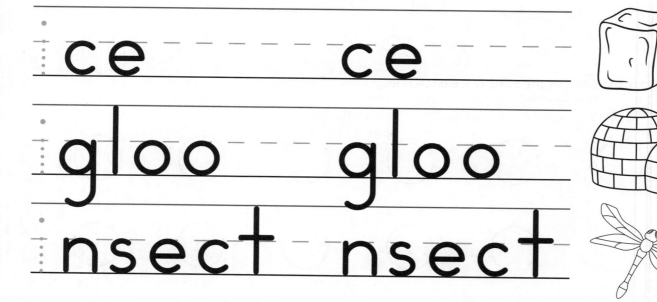

ce   ce

gloo   gloo

nsect   nsect

Directions: Trace the letters. Then, write the missing letter to complete each word.

130193—180 Days of Printing: Beginning

Name: _____

Directions: Start at the star. Trace each letter. Then, write your own letters to fill the lines.

sabel   sabel

van   van

ndia   ndia

Directions: Trace the letters. Then, write the missing letter to complete each name.

Activity

Name: _____

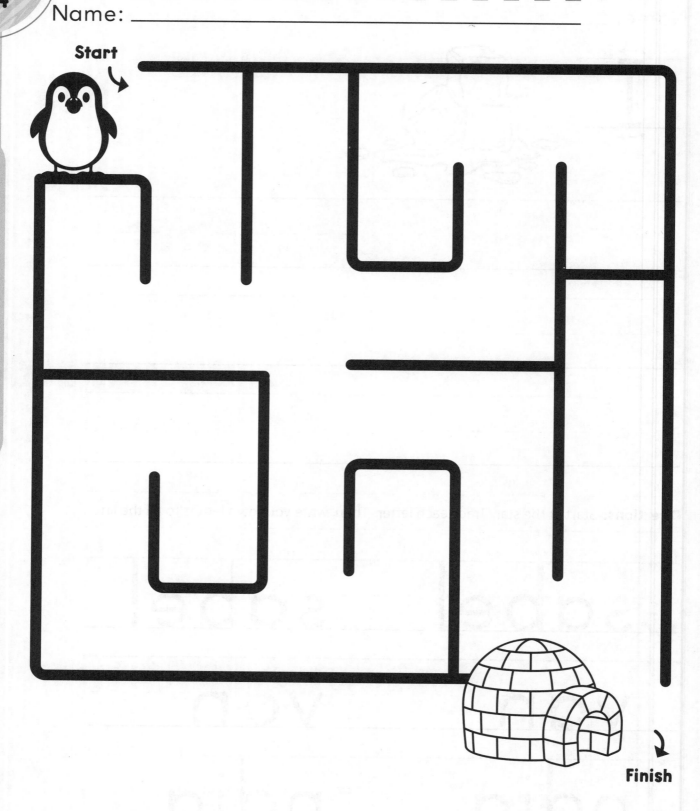

Directions: Use straight lines to help the penguin find his home through the maze.

Name: _____

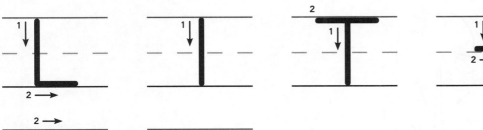
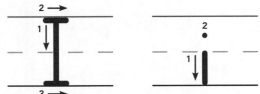
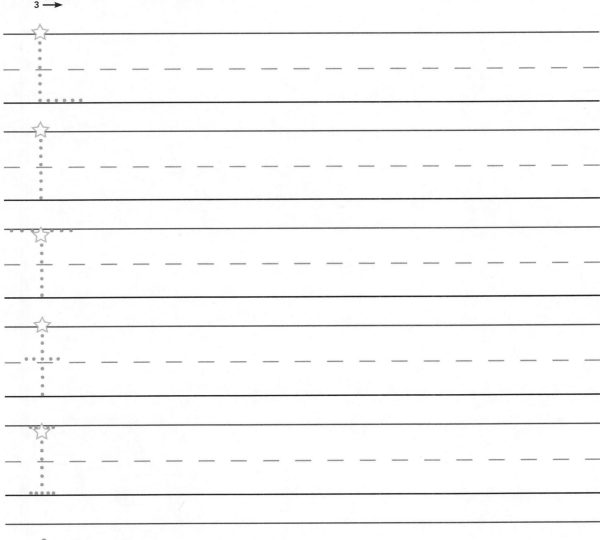

Directions: Trace the letters. Then, write your own letters to fill each line.

Name: _____

Directionality and Strokes

Directions: Start at the star. Trace each line.

130193—180 Days of Printing: Beginning

Name: _____

1 one

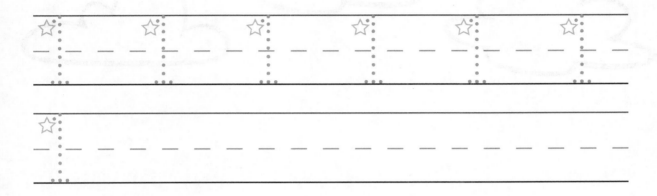

Directions: Start at the star. Trace each number. Then, write your own numbers to fill the line.

Directions: Count the objects. Trace the numbers. Then, write the missing numbers.

Print

Name: _____

Activity

Directions: Trace the rain. Then, use straight lines to draw more rain.

130193—180 Days of Printing: Beginning

Name: _____

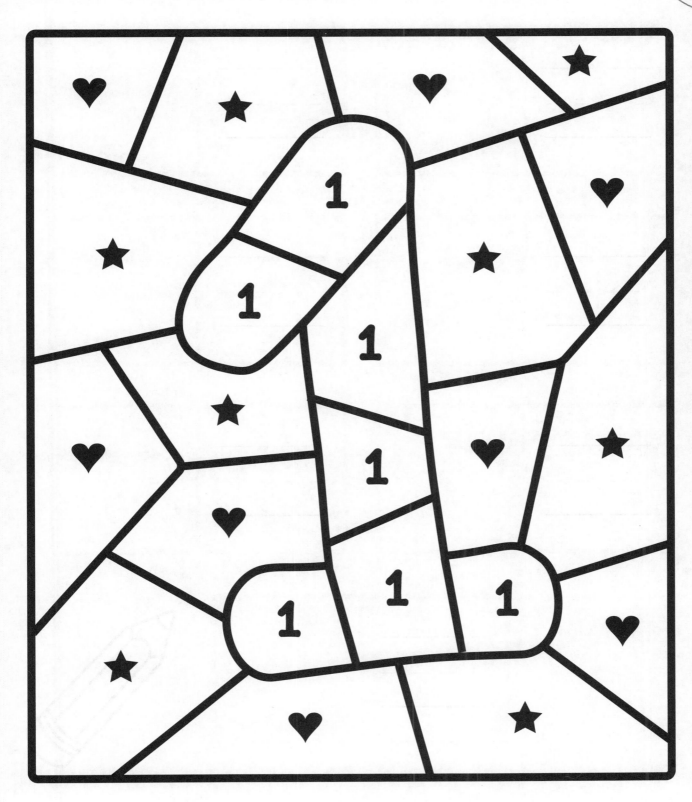

Directions: Use red to color each shape with a 1. Use a different color for each ♥ and ★.

Name: _____

Review

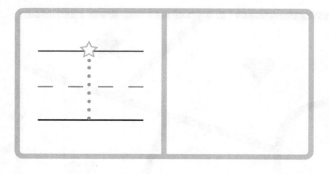

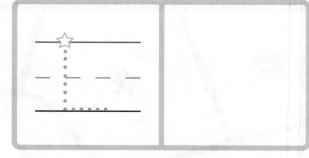

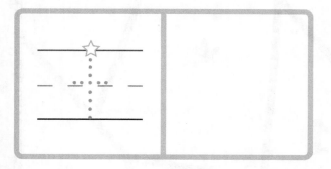

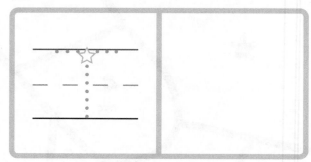

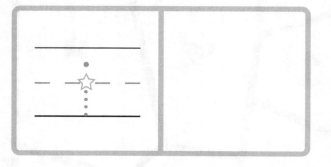

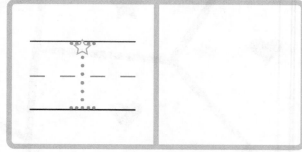

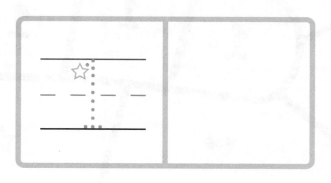

Directions: Trace each letter or number. Then, draw a picture that starts with the letter in each box. Draw one object in the box next to the 1.

Name: _____

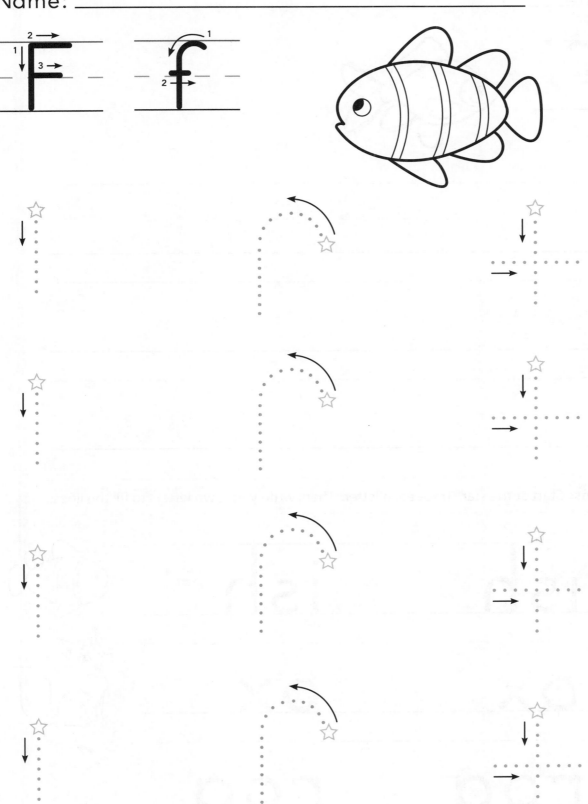

Directions: Start at the star. Connect the dots.

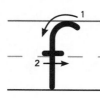

Name: _____

Print Lowercase

f

Directions: Start at the star. Trace each letter. Then, write your own letters to fill the lines.

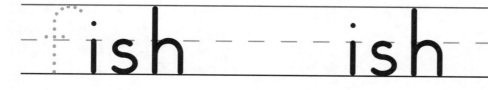

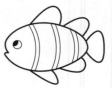

ish   ish

ox   ox

rog   rog

Directions: Trace the letters. Then, write the missing letter to complete each word.

Name: _____

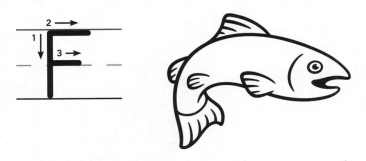

Directions: Start at the star. Trace each letter. Then, write your own letters to fill the lines.

red   red

riday   riday

lora   lora

Directions: Trace the letters. Then, write the missing letter to complete each name.

Name: _____

Activity

Directions: Connect the dots to complete the fish. Then, color the picture.

130193—180 Days of Printing: Beginning

Name: _____

Review

Directions: Trace the letters. Then, write your own letters to fill each line.

Name: _____

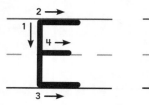 

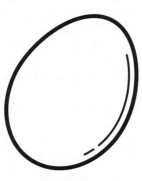

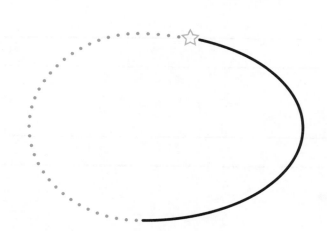

Directions: Start at the star. Connect the dots.

Name: _____

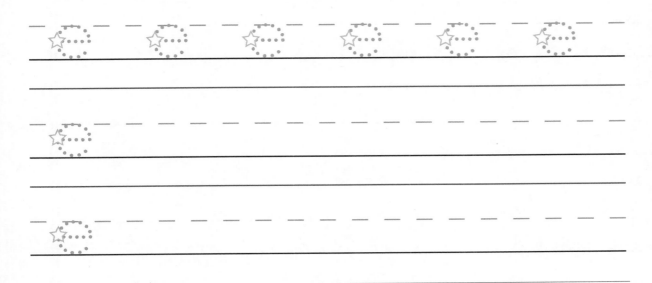

Print Lowercase

Directions: Start at the star. Trace each letter. Then, write your own letters to fill the lines.

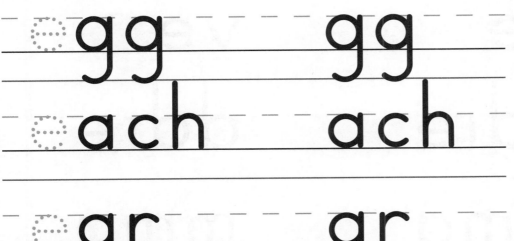

g g   g g

ach   ach

ar   ar

Directions: Trace the letters. Then, write the missing letter to complete each word.

Name: _____

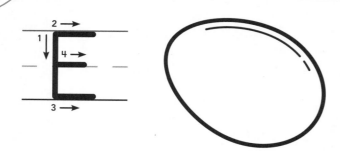

Print Uppercase

Directions: Start at the star. Trace each letter. Then, write your own letters to fill the lines.

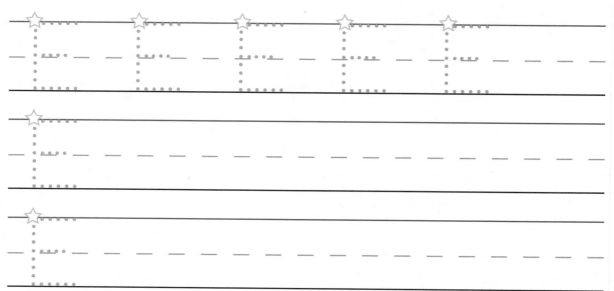

Directions: Trace the letters. Then, write the missing letter to complete each name.

Name: _____

Activity

Directions: Connect the little picture with the big picture. Practice writing without lifting your pencil.

Name: _____

I

i

f

F

e

E

Directions: Trace the letters. Then, write your own letters to fill each line.

Name: _____

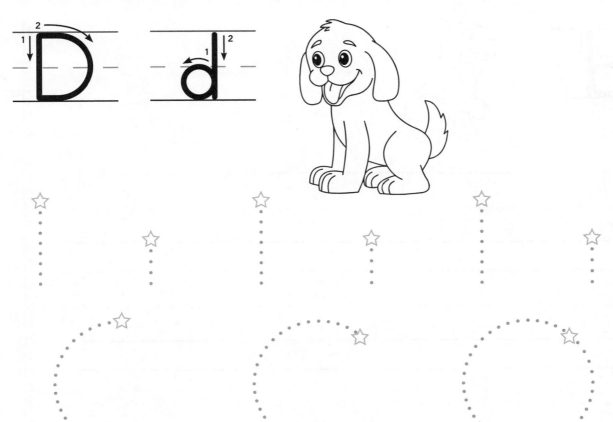

Directions: Start at the star. Connect the dots.

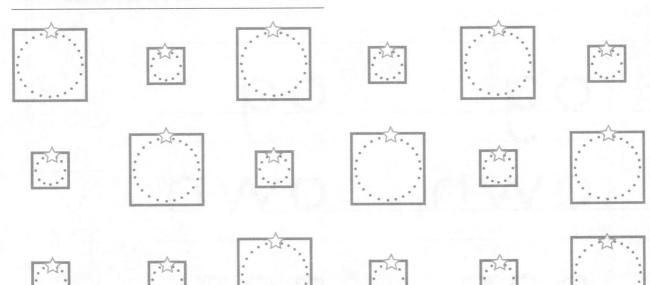

Directions: Draw circles in the squares.

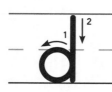

Name: _____

Print Lowercase

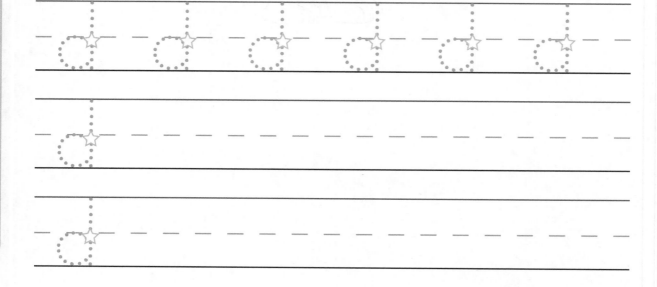

Directions: Start at the star. Trace each letter. Then, write your own letters to fill the lines.

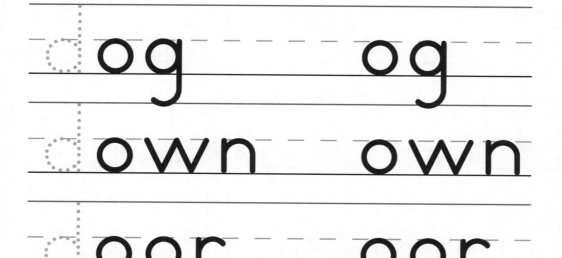

Directions: Trace the letters. Then, write the missing letter to complete each word.

Name: _____

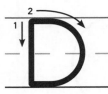
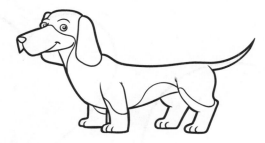

D D D D D

D

D

Directions: Start at the star. Trace each letter. Then, write your own letters to fill the lines.

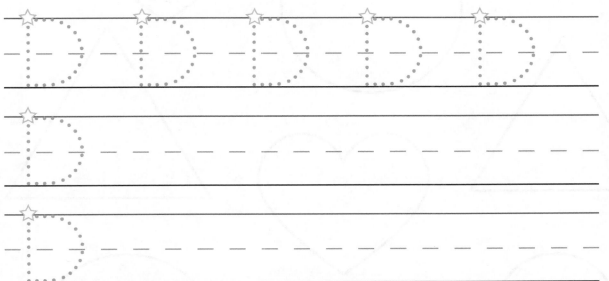

David   avid

Dora   ora

Daniel   aniel

Directions: Trace the letters. Then, write the missing letter to complete each name.

Activity

Name: _____

Directions: Write a *D* inside each heart and a *d* inside each triangle. Then, draw happy faces in the circles.

130193—180 Days of Printing: Beginning   © Shell Education

Name: _____

i

l

f

F

d

D

Directions: Trace the letters. Then, write your own letters to fill each line.

did

it

Directions: Trace the letters to write the words. Then, write each word two more times.

Name: _____

Directionality and Strokes

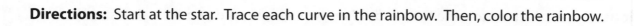

Directions: Start at the star. Trace each curve in the rainbow. Then, color the rainbow.

130193—180 Days of Printing: Beginning

Name: _____

2 two

Directions: Start at the star. Trace each number. Then, write your own numbers on the lines.

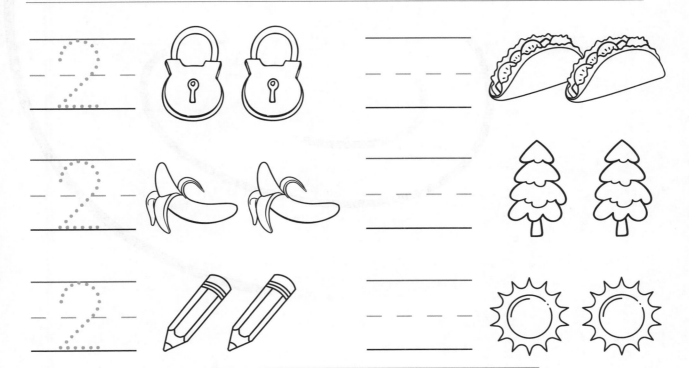

Directions: Count the objects. Trace the numbers. Then, write the numbers.

Print

Name: _____

Activity

Directions: Start at the star. Connect the dots. Then, color the duck two colors.

130193—180 Days of Printing: Beginning

© Shell Education

Name: _____

Activity

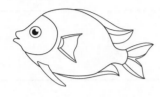

2

1

Directions: Count the animals. Write how many you see.

Name: _____

Review

a

E

i

l

t

2

Directions: Trace each letter or number. Then, write your own to fill each line.

at

Directions: Trace each letter to write the word. Then, write the word two more times.

Name: _____

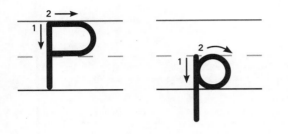 

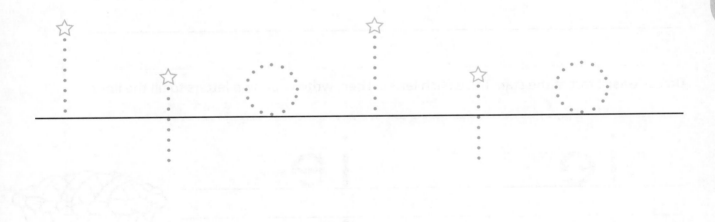

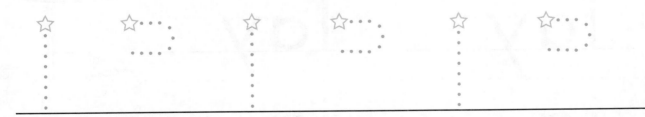

Directions: Start at the star. Connect the dots.

Print Lowercase

Name: _____

p

p p p p p p

p

p

Directions: Start at the star. Trace each letter. Then, write your own letters to fill the lines.

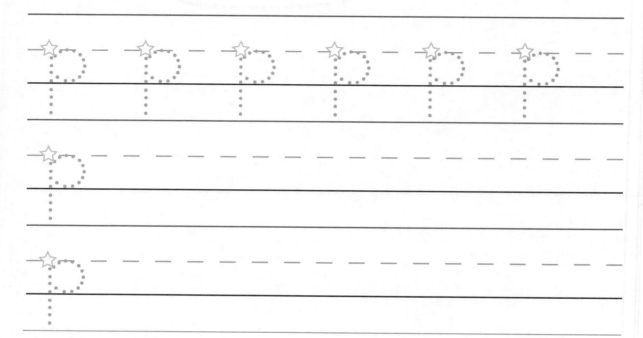

pie   ie

play   lay

pig   ig

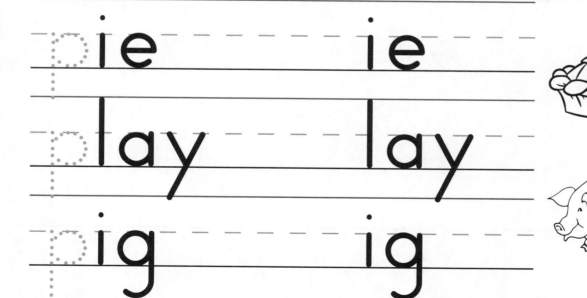

Directions: Trace the letters. Then, write the missing letter to complete each word.

Name: _____

Directions: Start at the star. Trace each letter. Then, write your own letters to fill the lines.

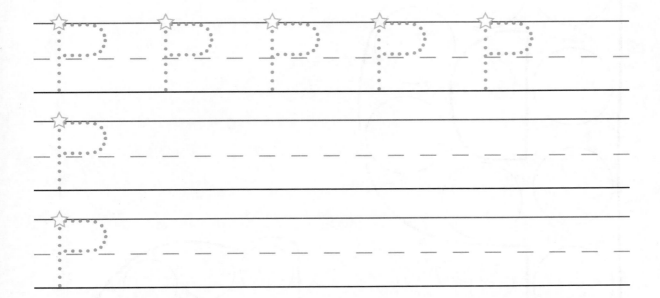

P am   am

P riya   riya

P aul   aul

Directions: Trace the letters. Then, write the missing letter to complete each name.

Name: _____

Activity

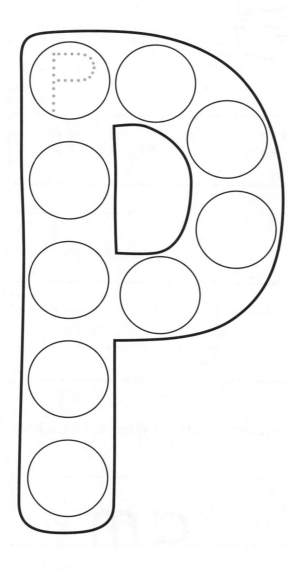

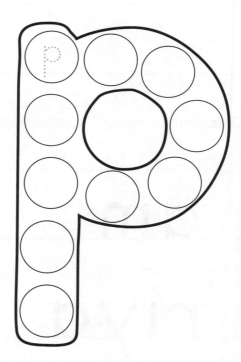

Directions: Write the uppercase or lowercase letter in the polka dots. Color the letters.

130193—180 Days of Printing: Beginning

Name: _____

P

P

d

D

Directions: Trace the letters. Then, write your own letters to fill each line.

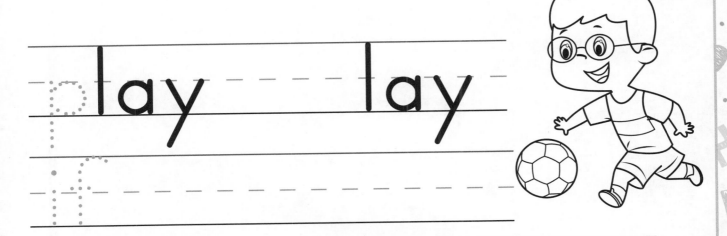

play   lay

Directions: Trace the letters. Then, write the missing letter to complete the word. Write the word two more times.

Name:

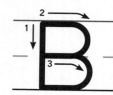 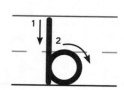

Directionality and Strokes

Directions: Start at the star. Connect the dots.

Name: _____

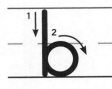

☆ b b b b b b

☆ b

☆ b

Directions: Start at the star. Trace each letter. Then, write your own letters to fill the lines.

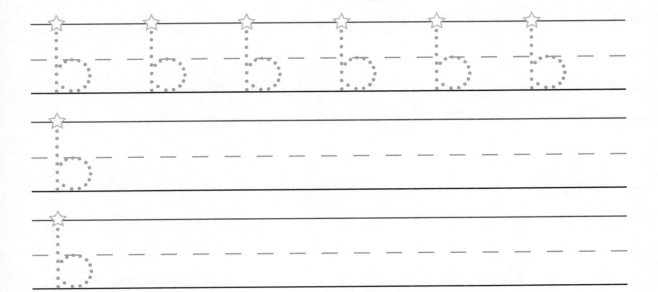

bear   ear

big   ig

bag   ag

Directions: Trace the letters. Then, write the missing letter to complete each word.

Print Uppercase

Name: _____

Directions: Start at the star. Trace each letter. Then, write your own letters to fill the lines.

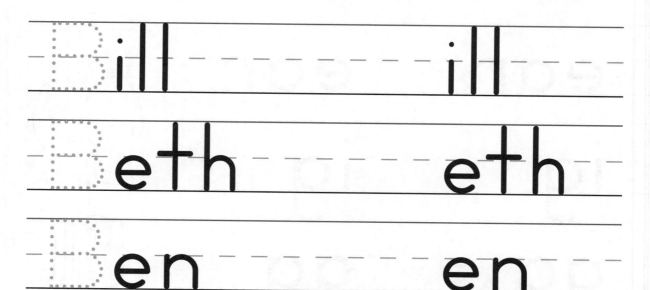

Directions: Trace the letters. Then, write the missing letter to complete each name.

p ⎯⎯⎯⎯⎯⎯⎯ L

b   P

d   D

I   B

Directions: Match the lowercase letter to the uppercase letter.

Review

Name: _____

b _____

B _____

e _____

E _____

Directions: Trace the letters. Then, write your own letters to fill each line.

big   ig

be

Directions: Trace the letters. Then, write the letter to complete the word. Write the word two more times.

130193—180 Days of Printing: Beginning   © Shell Education

Name: _____

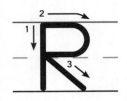 

Directions: Start at each star. Connect the dots.

Name: _____

Print Lowercase

Directions: Start at the star. Trace each letter. Then, write your own letters to fill the lines.

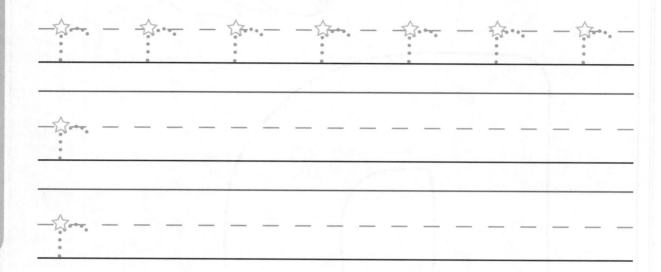

r abbit   abbit

r un   un

r ain   ain

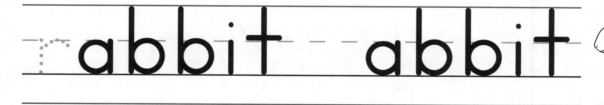
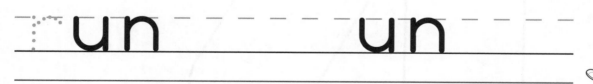

Directions: Trace the letters. Then, write the missing letter to complete each word.

Name: _____

Directions: Start at the star. Trace each letter. Then, write your own letters to fill the lines.

R yan   yan

R achel   achel

R hea   hea

Directions: Trace the letters. Then, write the missing letter to complete each name.

Name: _____

Activity

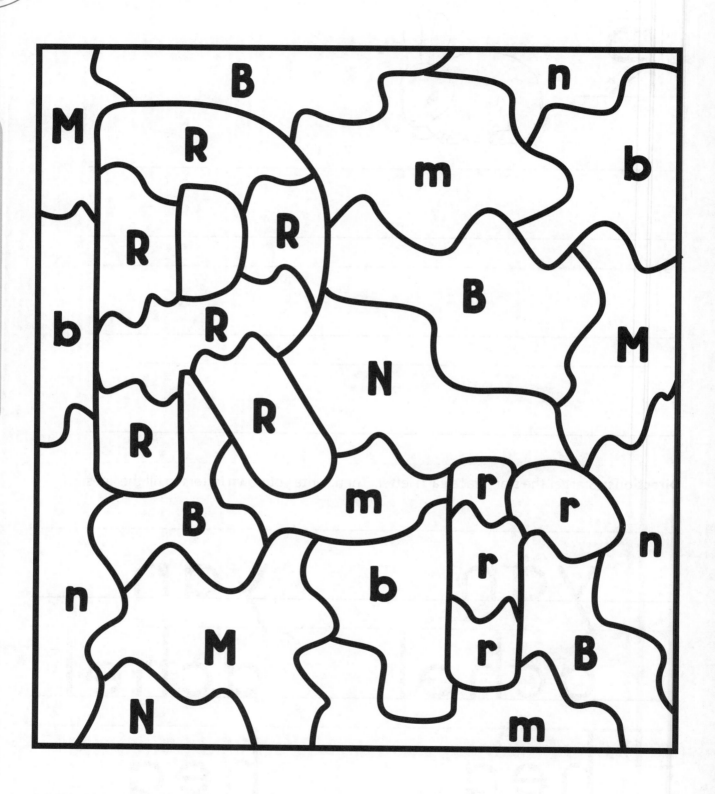

Directions: Color the shapes with *R* and *r* blue. Use different colors for the other letters.

130193—180 Days of Printing: Beginning

Name: _____

I

T

D

B

Directions: Trace each letter. Then, write your own letters to fill each line.

Tuesday

uesday

red

Directions: Trace the letters. Then, write the missing letter to complete the word. Write the word two more times.

130193—180 Days of Printing: Beginning

Name:

Directionality and Strokes

Directions: Start at the star. Connect the dots.

130193—180 Days of Printing: Beginning

© Shell Education

Name: _____

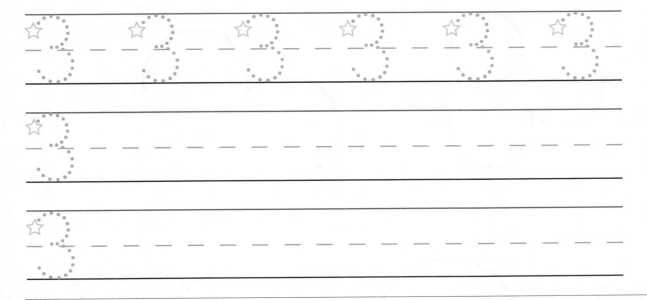

Print

Directions: Start at the star. Trace each number. Then, write your own numbers on the lines.

Directions: Count the objects. Trace the numbers. Then, write the numbers.

Name: _____

Activity

Directions: Trace each curve and circle to finish the flowers. Color the flowers.

130193—180 Days of Printing: Beginning

Name: _____

Activity

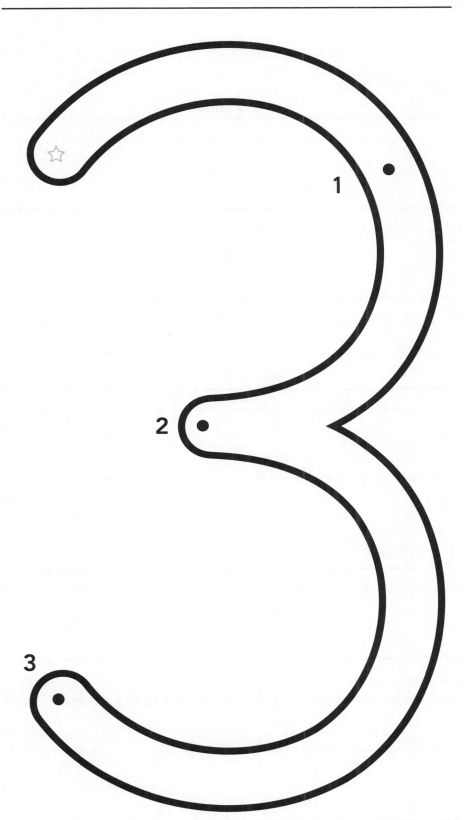

Directions: Start at the star. Connect the dots. Count as you write.

Review

Name: _____

T - - - - - - - - - - - - - - - - - - -

R - - - - - - - - - - - - - - - - - - -

b - - - - - - - - - - - - - - - - - - -

B - - - - - - - - - - - - - - - - - - -

1 - - - - - - - - - - - - - - - - - - -

2 - - - - - - - - - - - - - - - - - - -

3 - - - - - - - - - - - - - - - - - - -

Directions: Trace each letter or number. Then, write your own to fill each line.

be - - - - - - - - - - - - - - - - - -

Directions: Trace each letter to write the word. Then, write the word two more times.

130193—180 Days of Printing: Beginning

Name: _____

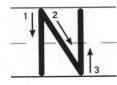 

Directions: Start at the star. Trace each line.

Print Lowercase

Name: _____

n

n n n n n n

n

n

Directions: Start at the star. Trace each letter. Then, write your own letters to fill the lines.

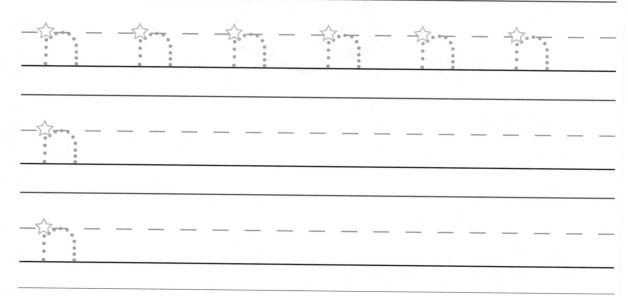

nose   ose

no   o

number   umber

Directions: Trace the letters. Then, write the missing letter to complete each word.

Name: _____

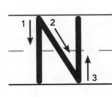 

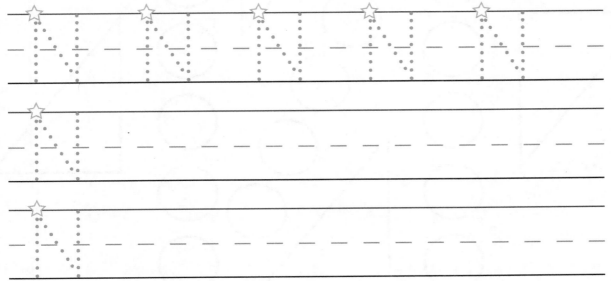

Directions: Start at the star. Trace each letter. Then, write your own letters to fill the lines.

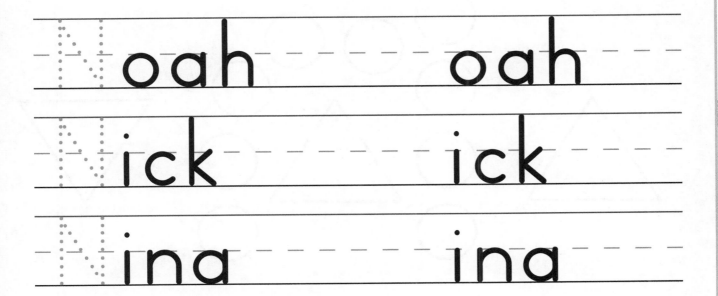

Directions: Trace the letters. Then, write the missing letter to complete each name.

Print Uppercase

Name: _____

Activity

Directions: Color the circles blue. Then, color the triangles green. What letter do you see?

130193—180 Days of Printing: Beginning

© Shell Education

Name: _____

n

i

e

f

Directions: Trace each letter. Then, write your own letters to fill each line.

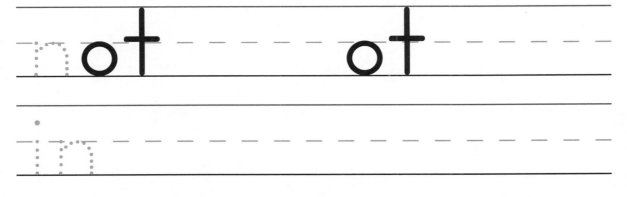

not   ot

in

Directions: Trace the letters. Then, write the missing letter to complete the word. Write the word two more times.

Name: _____

Directionality and Strokes

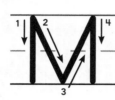 

Directions: Start at the star. Connect the dots.

130193—180 Days of Printing: Beginning
© Shell Education

Name: _____

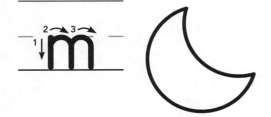

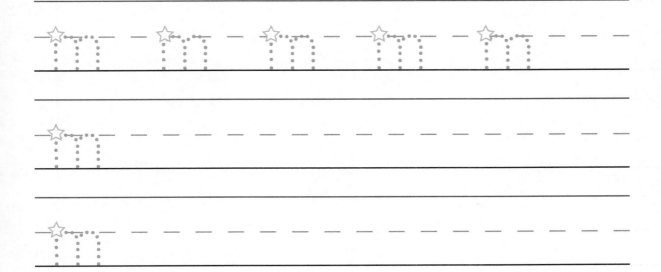

Directions: Start at the star. Trace each letter. Then, write your own letters to fill the lines.

moon   oon

me   e

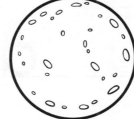

man   an

Directions: Trace the letters. Then, write the missing letter to complete each word.

Name: _____

Print Uppercase

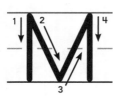

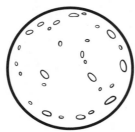

Directions: Start at the star. Trace each letter. Then, write your own letters to fill the lines.

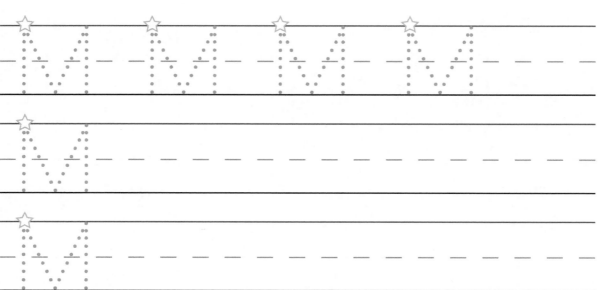

Mary   ary

aya   aya

att   att

Directions: Trace the letters. Then, write the missing letter to complete each name.

Name: _____

Activity

Directions: Use straight lines to help the monkey get to the tree.

WEEK 14
DAY
5

Name: _____

Review

Directions: Trace the letters. Then, write your own letters to fill each line.

more   ore

me

Directions: Trace the letters. Then, write the missing letter to complete the word. Write the word two more times.

82   130193—180 Days of Printing: Beginning   © Shell Education

Name: _____

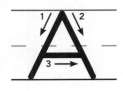 

Directions: Start at the star. Trace each line.

Name: _____

Print Lowercase

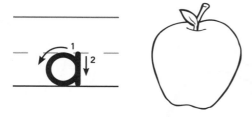

a

☆ ☆ ☆ ☆ ☆ ☆

☆

☆

Directions: Start at the star. Trace each letter. Then, write your own letters to fill the lines.

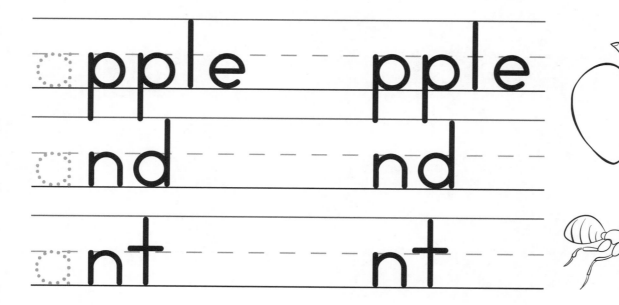

apple   apple

and   and

ant   ant

Directions: Trace the letters. Then, write the missing letter to complete each word.

Name: _____

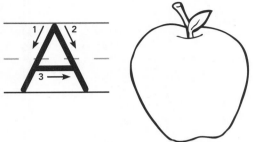

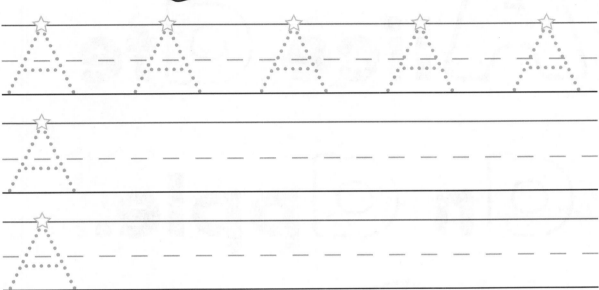

Directions: Start at the star. Trace each letter. Then, write your own letters to fill the lines.

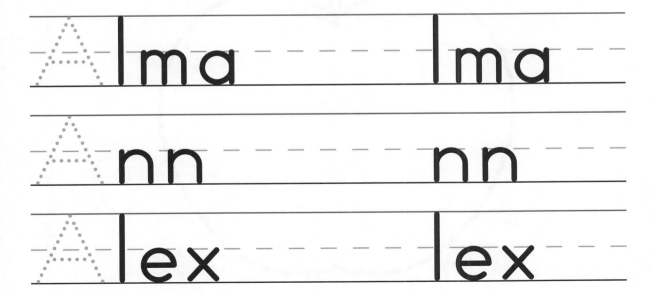

Directions: Trace the letters. Then, write the missing letter to complete each name.

Name: _____

Activity

Directions: Trace each *A* and *a*. Then, decorate the letters and color the apple.

130193—180 Days of Printing: Beginning

Name: _____

i _____

I _____

f _____

F _____

Directions: Trace each letter. Then, write your own letters to fill each line.

A lyssa   lyssa

fi sh   sh

Directions: Trace the letters. Then, write the missing letters to complete each word or name.

Directionality and Strokes

Name: _____

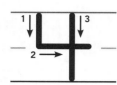

Directions: Start at the star. Trace each line.

130193—180 Days of Printing: Beginning

Name: _____

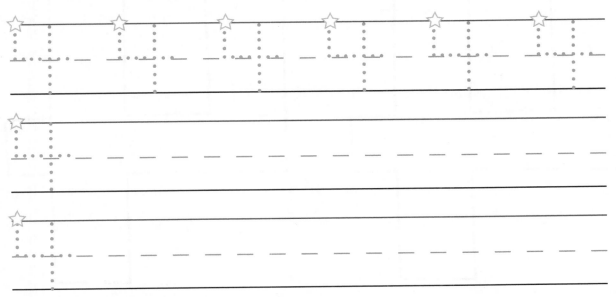

Directions: Start at the star. Trace each number. Then, write your own numbers on the lines.

Directions: Count the objects. Trace the numbers. Then, write the numbers.

Name: _____

Activity

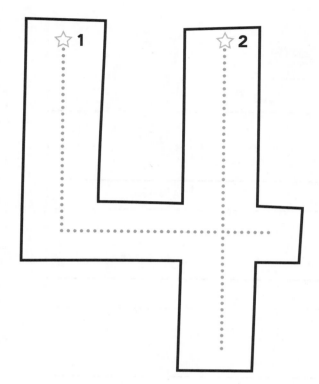

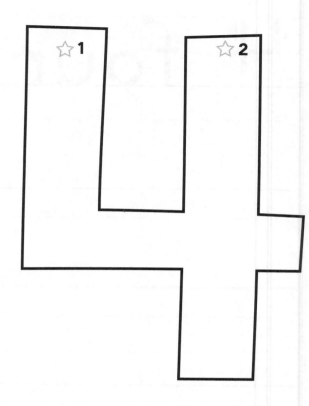

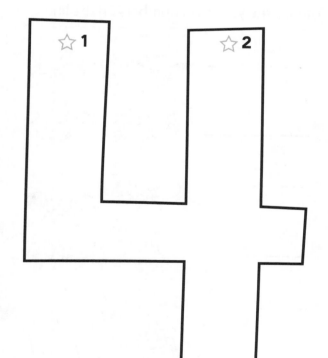

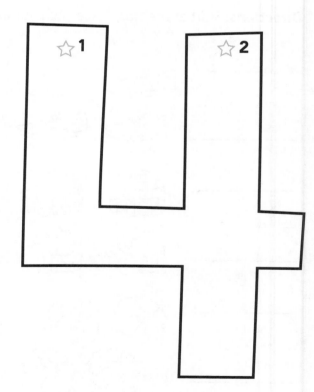

Directions: Write the number in the outlines. Color each 4 a different color.

130193—180 Days of Printing: Beginning

Name: _____

Directions: Write a 4 in each shape. Color the shapes different colors.

Review

Name: _____

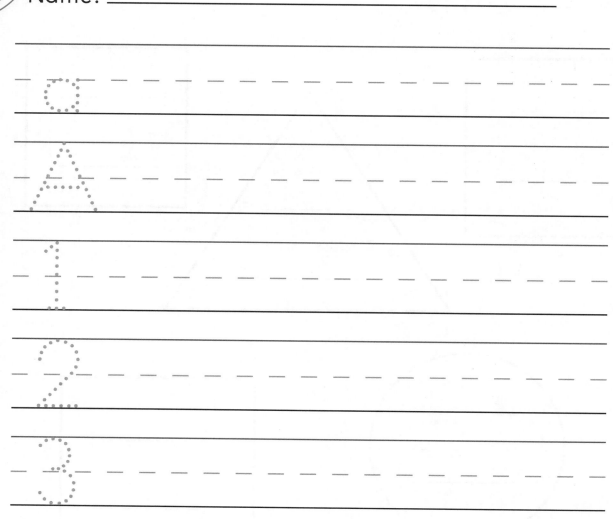

O

A

1

2

3

I

Directions: Trace each letter or number. Then, write your own to fill each line.

me

Directions: Trace each letter to write the word. Then, write the word two more times.

130193—180 Days of Printing: Beginning
© Shell Education

Name: _____

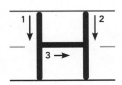 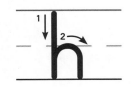

Directions: Start at the star. Trace each stroke.

Name: _____

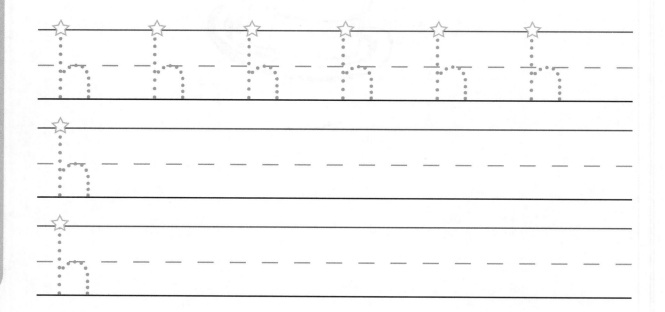

Directions: Start at the star. Trace each letter. Then, write your own letters to fill the lines.

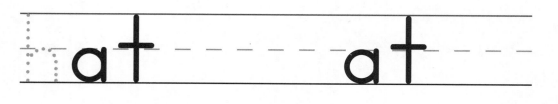

Directions: Trace the letters. Then, write the missing letter to complete each word.

Name: _____

Directions: Start at the star. Trace each letter. Then, write your own letters to fill the lines.

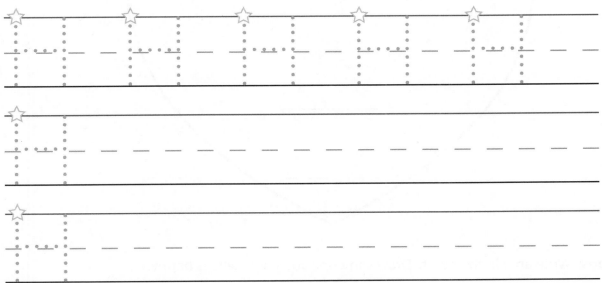

Directions: Trace the letters. Then, write the missing letter to complete each name.

Activity

Name: _____

Directions: Write an *H* in the heart. Draw someone you know who is happy.

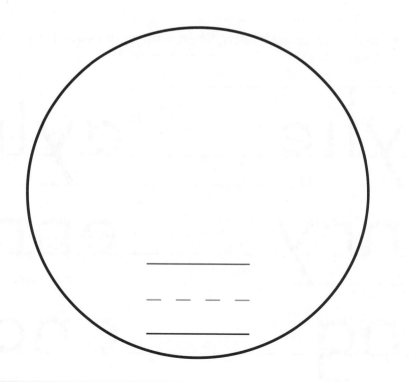

Directions: Write an *h* in the circle. Draw something you like that starts with *h*.

Name: _____

e _____

E _____

d _____

D _____

Directions: Trace each letter. Then, write your own letters to fill each line.

happy   appy

the

Directions: Trace each letter. Then, write the missing letter to complete the word. Write the word two more times.

Name: _____

 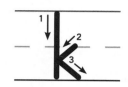

Directionality and Strokes

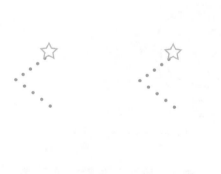 

Directions: Start at the star. Trace each line.

130193—180 Days of Printing: Beginning

Name: _____

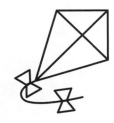

Directions: Start at the star. Trace each letter. Then, write your own letters to fill the lines.

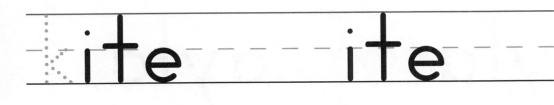

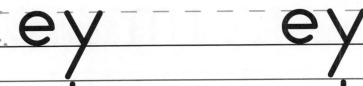

Directions: Trace the letters. Then, write the missing letter to complete each word.

Name: _____

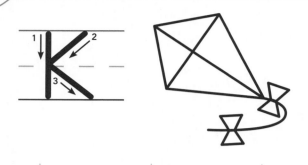

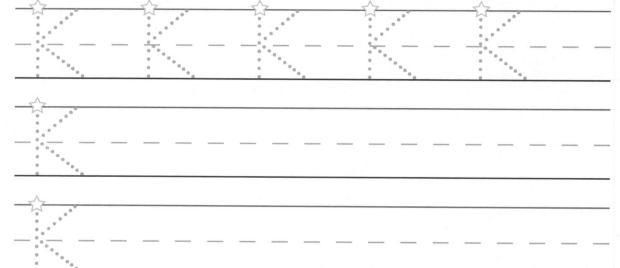

Print Uppercase

Directions: Start at the star. Trace each letter. Then, write your own letters to fill the lines.

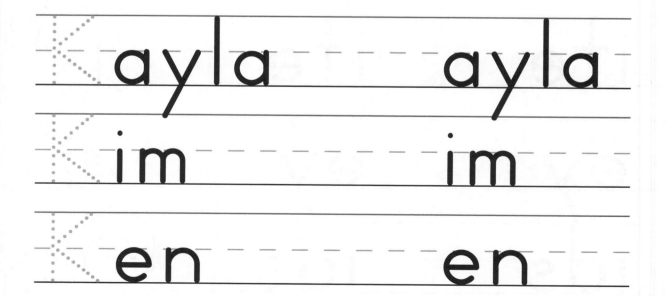

ayla   ayla

im   im

en   en

Directions: Trace the letters. Then, write the missing letter to complete each name.

130193—180 Days of Printing: Beginning

Name: _____

Directions: Trace each line. Then, color the picture.

Name: _____

Review

P

P

b

B

Directions: Trace each letter. Then, write your own letters to fill each line.

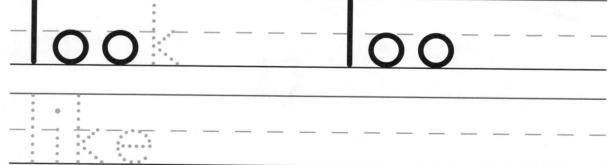

look   loo

like

Directions: Trace each letter. Then, write the missing letter to complete the word. Write the word two more times.

Name: _____

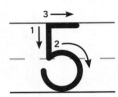

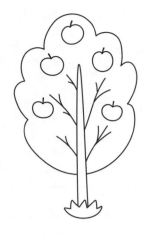

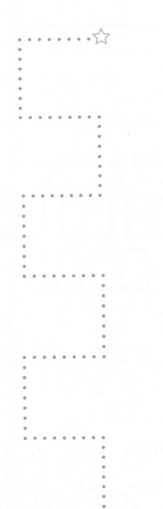

Directions: Start at the star. Connect the dots.

Name: _____

Print

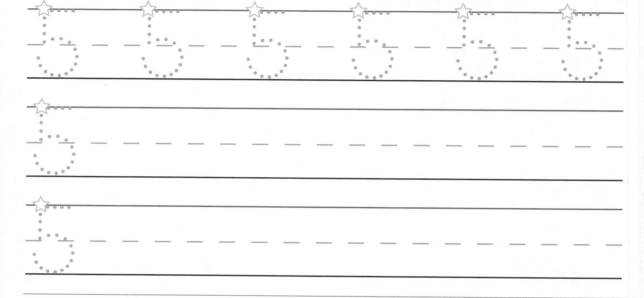

Directions: Start at the star. Trace each number. Then, write your own numbers on the lines.

Directions: Count the objects. Trace the numbers. Then, write the numbers.

Name: _____

Activity

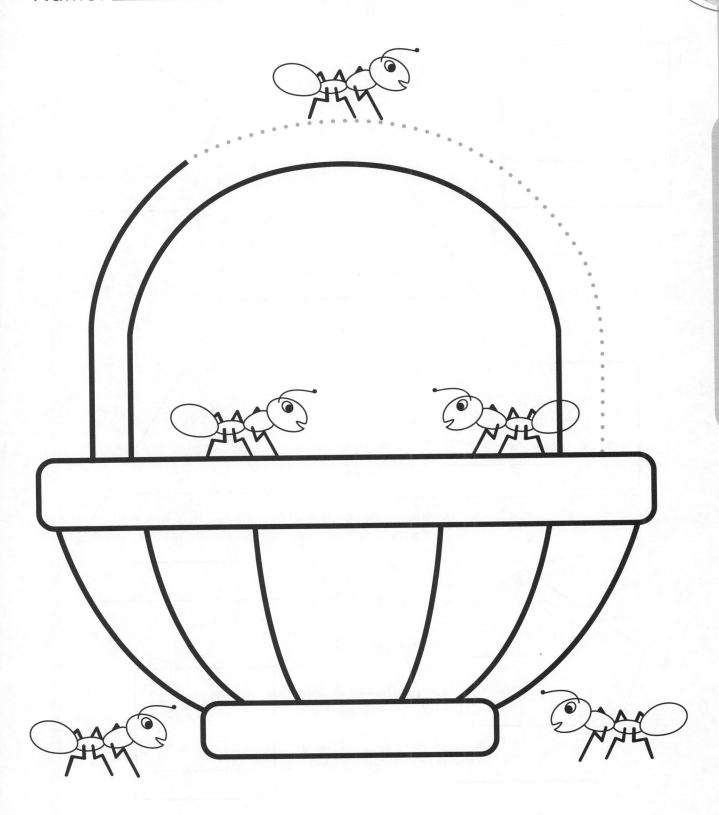

Directions: Connect the dots. Count the ants. Then, color the picture.

Name: _____

Activity

Directions: Count the sides of the shapes. Then, write the number of sides in each shape.

130193—180 Days of Printing: Beginning

© Shell Education

Name: _____

1 -

2 -

3 -

4 -

5 -

Review

Directions: Trace each number. Then, write your own to fill each line.

I have

apples.

Directions: Count the apples. Write the number of apples in the sentence.

Name: _____

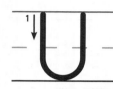 

Directionality and Strokes

☆ ☆ ☆

Directions: Start at the star. Trace each curve.

Name: _____

1↓u↓2

☆ u   ☆ u   ☆ u   ☆ u   ☆ u   ☆ u

☆ u

☆ u

Directions: Start at the star. Trace each letter. Then, write your own letters to fill the lines.

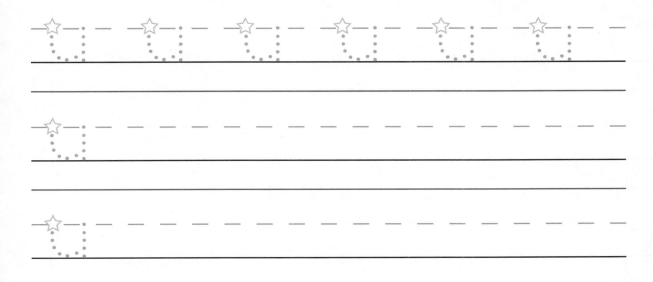

umbrella   umbrella

up   up

under   under

Directions: Trace the letters. Then, write the missing letter to complete each word.

Print Uppercase

Name: _____

Directions: Start at the star. Trace each letter. Then, write your own letters to fill the lines.

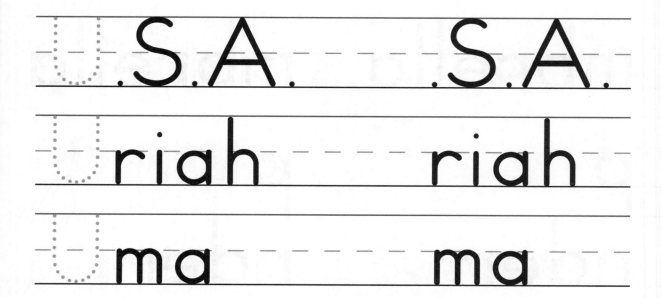

Directions: Trace the letters. Then, write the missing letter to complete each name.

Activity

Directions: Trace each curve. Then, color the picture.

Review

Name: _____

r

R

n

N

Directions: Trace each letter. Then, write your own letters to fill each line.

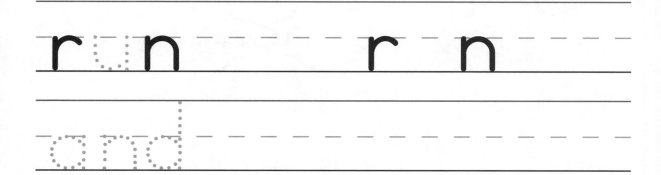

r u n   r   n

a n d

Directions: Trace each letter. Then, write the missing letter to complete the word. Write the word two more times.

Name: _____

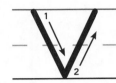 

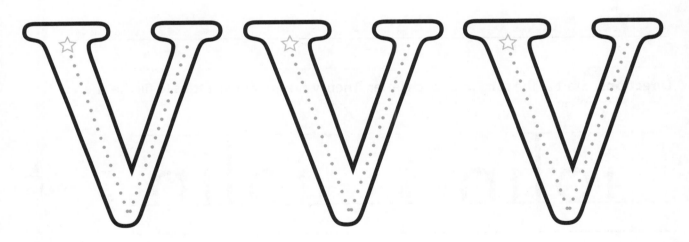

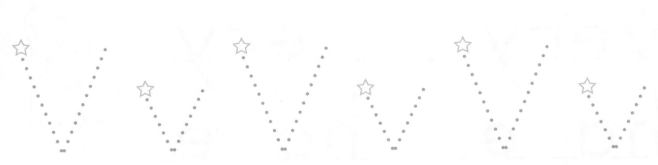

Directions: Start at the star. Trace each line.

Print Lowercase

Name: _____

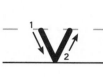

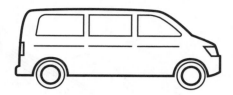

Directions: Start at the star. Trace each letter. Then, write your own letters to fill the lines.

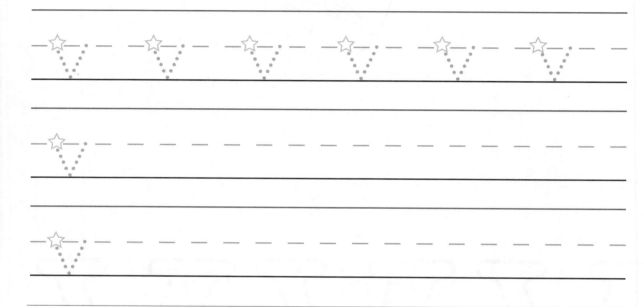

violin   iolin

very   ery

have   ha e

Directions: Trace the letters. Then, write the missing letter to complete each word.

Name: _____

Directions: Start at the star. Trace each letter. Then, write your own letters to fill the lines.

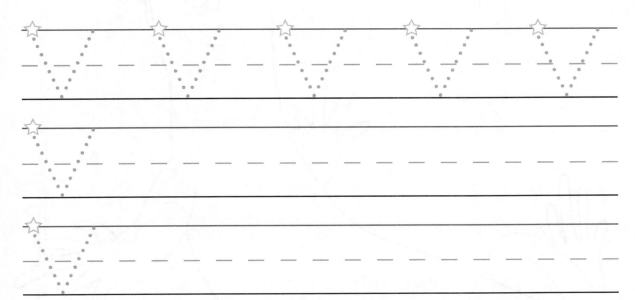

Valeria   aleria

Vernon   ernon

Victor   ictor

Directions: Trace the letters. Then, write the missing letter to complete each name.

    130193—180 Days of Printing: Beginning

Name: _____

Activity

Directions: Trace each line. Then, color the picture.

130193—180 Days of Printing: Beginning

Name: _____

E

M

c

A

Directions: Trace each letter. Then, write your own letters to fill each line.

have ha e

at

Directions: Trace each letter. Then, write the missing letter to complete the word. Write the word two more times.

Directionality and Strokes

Name: _____

Directions: Start at the star. Connect the dots.

130193—180 Days of Printing: Beginning

Name: _____

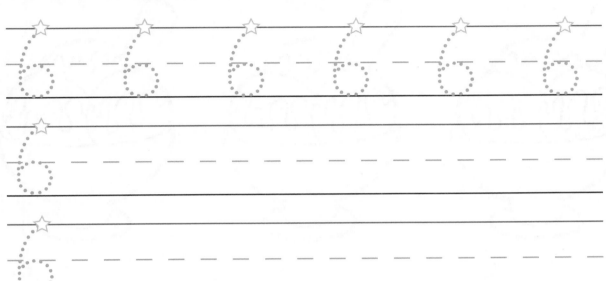

6 six

Directions: Start at the star. Trace each number. Then, write your own numbers on the lines.

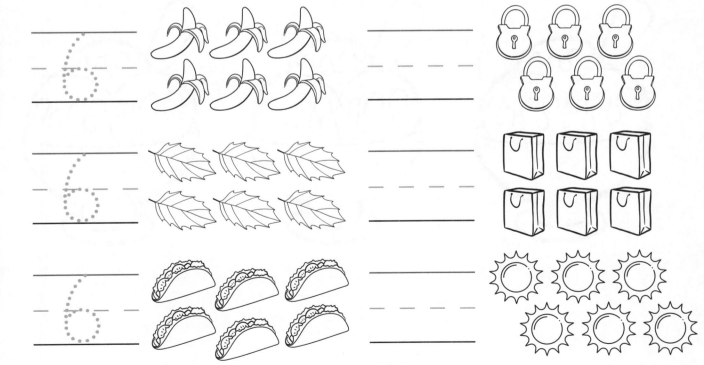

Directions: Count the objects. Trace the numbers. Then, write the numbers.

Print

Name: _____

Directions: Connect the dots. Count how many. Then, color the pictures.

130193—180 Days of Printing: Beginning

Name: _____

Activity

1

2

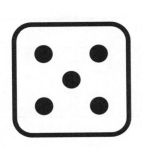

3

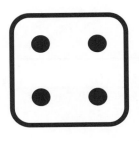

4

5

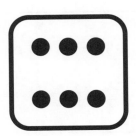

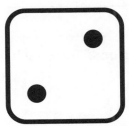

6

Directions: Count the dots. Draw a line to match the dots to the number.

Name: _____

1

2

3

4

5

6

Directions: Trace each number. Then, write your own to fill each line.

I am ____ years old.

Directions: How old are you? Write your age in the sentence.

Name: _____

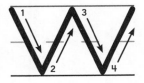 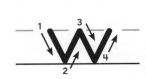 

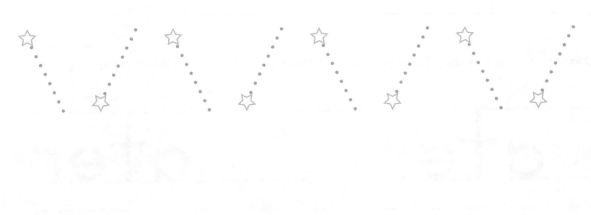

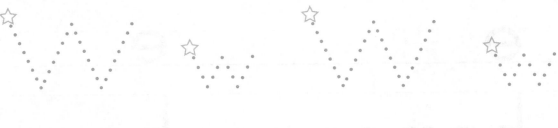

Directions: Start at the star. Trace each line.

Name: _____

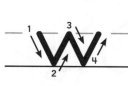

Print Lowercase

w   w   w   w

w

w

Directions: Start at the star. Trace each letter. Then, write your own letters to fill the lines.

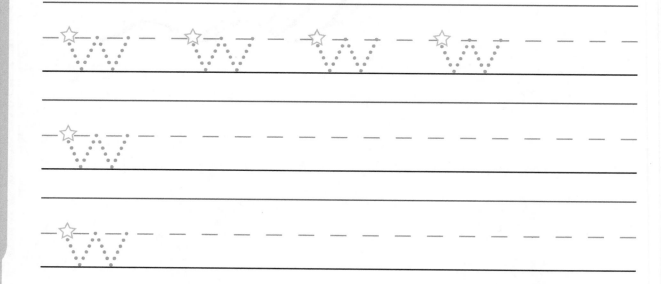

water   ater

we   e

where   here

Directions: Trace the letters. Then, write the missing letter to complete each word.

130193—180 Days of Printing: Beginning   © Shell Education

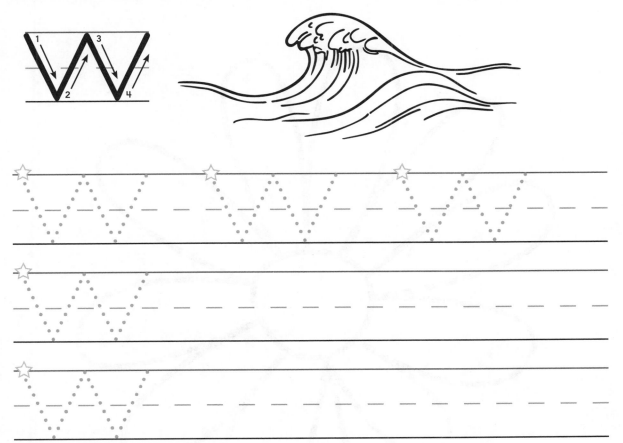

Directions: Start at the star. Trace each letter. Then, write your own letters to fill the lines.

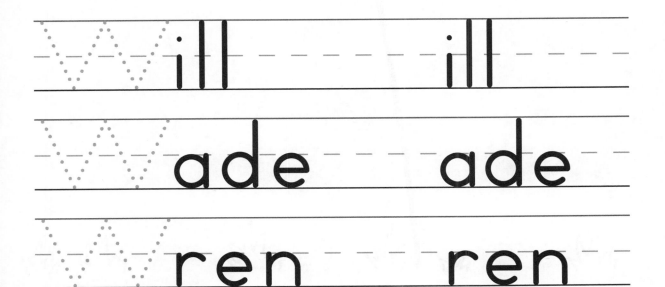

Directions: Trace the letters. Then, write the missing letter to complete each name.

Name: _____

Activity

Directions: Trace each line. Add more grass to the picture. Then, color the picture.

Name: _____

Review

h

H

k

K

Directions: Trace each letter. Then, write your own letters to fill each line.

water   ater

said

Directions: Trace each letter. Then, write the missing letter to complete the word. Write the word two more times.

Name: _____

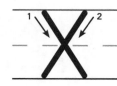 

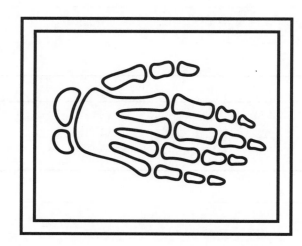

Directionality and Strokes

Directions: Start at the star. Trace each line.

Name: _____

Print Lowercase

Directions: Start at the star. Trace each letter. Then, write your own letters to fill the lines.

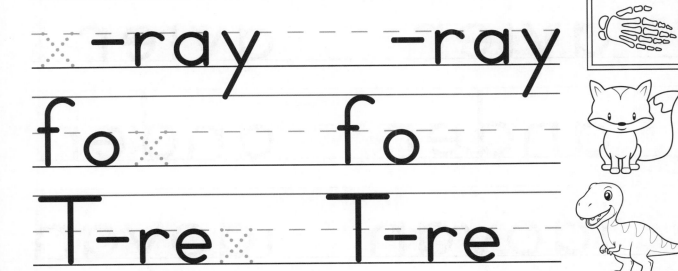

x-ray   -ray

fo   fo

T-re   T-re

Directions: Trace the letters. Then, write the missing letter to complete each word.

© Shell Education   130193—180 Days of Printing: Beginning   129

Print Uppercase

Name: _____

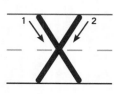

Directions: Start at the star. Trace each letter. Then, write your own letters to fill the lines.

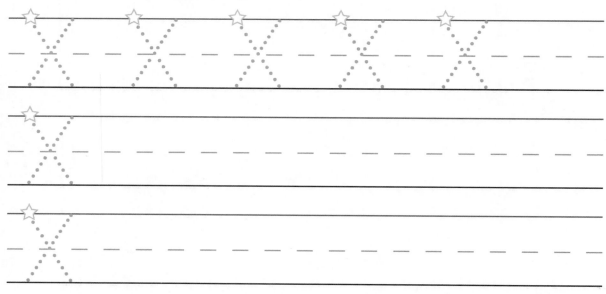

Directions: Trace the letters. Then, write the missing letter to complete each name.

130193—180 Days of Printing: Beginning

© Shell Education

Name: _____

N	K	H	K	K	Y	K
X	Y	N	K	H	K	X
K	X	K	H	Y	X	Y
Y	K	X	K	X	N	N
N	K	H	X	K	Y	Y
K	H	X	Y	X	H	K
Y	X	K	H	N	X	Y
X	K	K	Y	Y	N	X
N	Y	H	K	H	K	K

Directions: Color the squares with *X* green. Then, color the remaining letters yellow. What letter do you see?

Name: _____

Review

Directions: Trace each letter. Then, write your own letters to fill each line.

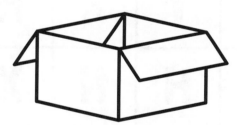

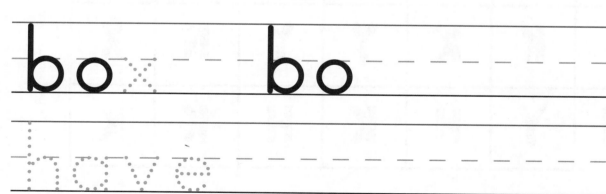

Directions: Trace each letter. Then, write the missing letter to complete the word. Write the word two more times.

Name: _____

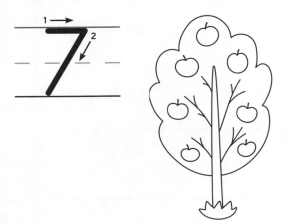

Directionality and Strokes

Directions: Start at the star. Trace each line.

Name:

7 seven

Directions: Start at the star. Trace each number. Then, write your own numbers on the lines.

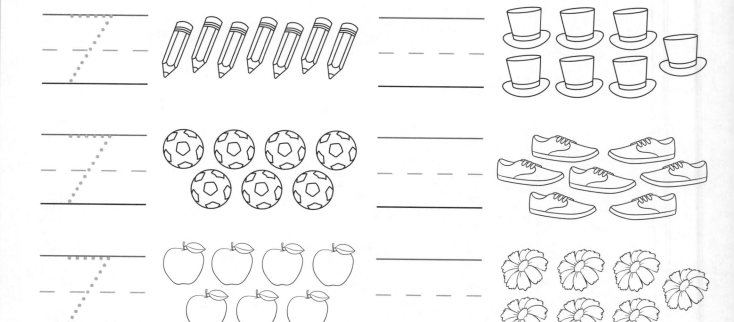

Directions: Count the objects. Trace the numbers. Then, write the numbers.

Activity

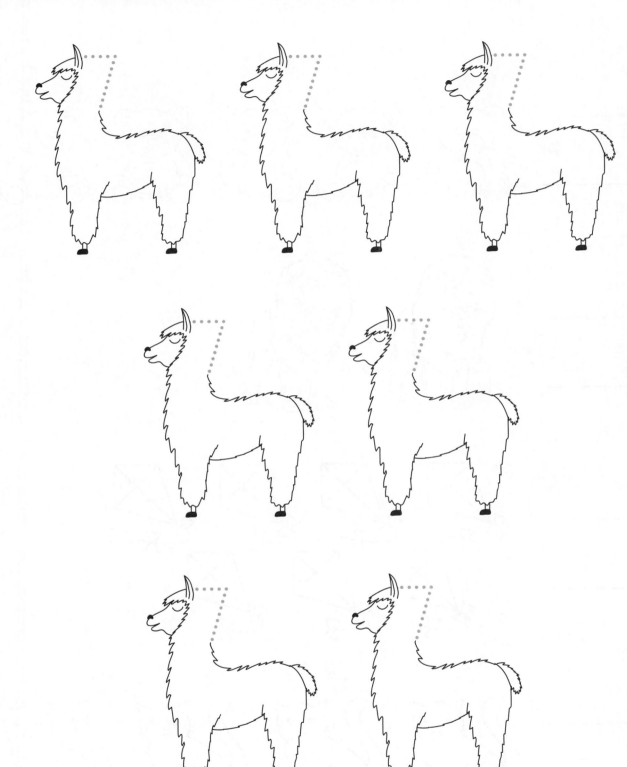

Directions: Trace each line. Count how many. Then, color the animals different colors.

Activity

Name: _____

_____
- - - - - - - - - - - -
_____

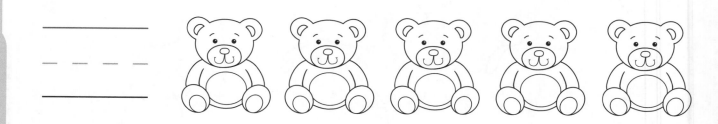

_____
- - - - - - - - - - - -
_____

_____
- - - - - - - - - - - -
_____

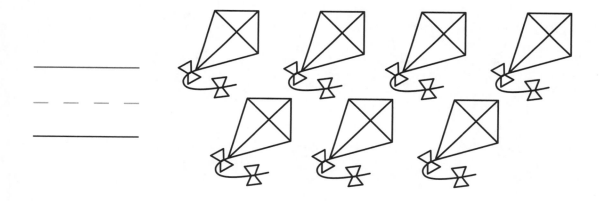

_____
- - - - - - - - - - - -
_____

Directions: Count how many items you see. Then, write the number.

130193—180 Days of Printing: Beginning

Name: _____

1

2

3

4

5

6

7

Directions: Trace each number. Then, write your own to fill each line.

I see ____ rabbits.

Directions: How many rabbits do you see? Write the number in the sentence.

Name: _____

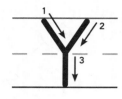

Directionality and Strokes

Directions: Start at the star. Trace each line.

130193—180 Days of Printing: Beginning

© Shell Education

Name: _____

y

☆y - ☆y - ☆y - ☆y - ☆y - ☆y

☆y

☆y

Print Lowercase

Directions: Start at the star. Trace each letter. Then, write your own letters to fill the lines.

yarn   arn

m   m

to   to

Directions: Trace the letters. Then, write the missing letter to complete each word.

Print Uppercase

Name: _____

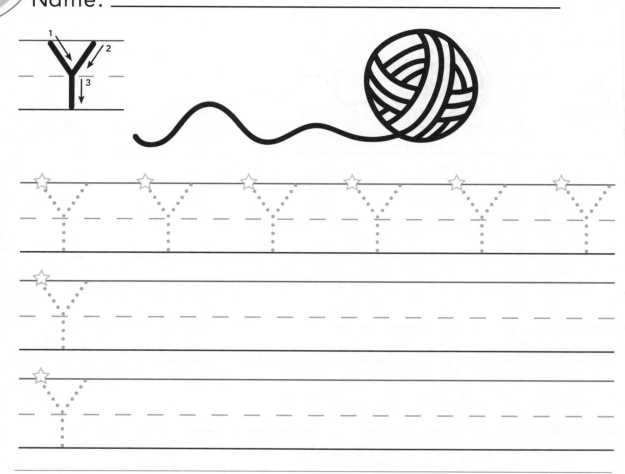

Directions: Start at the star. Trace each letter. Then, write your own letters to fill the lines.

ara   ara

vonne   vonne

an   an

Directions: Trace the letters. Then, write the missing letter to complete each name.

130193—180 Days of Printing: Beginning

Name: _____

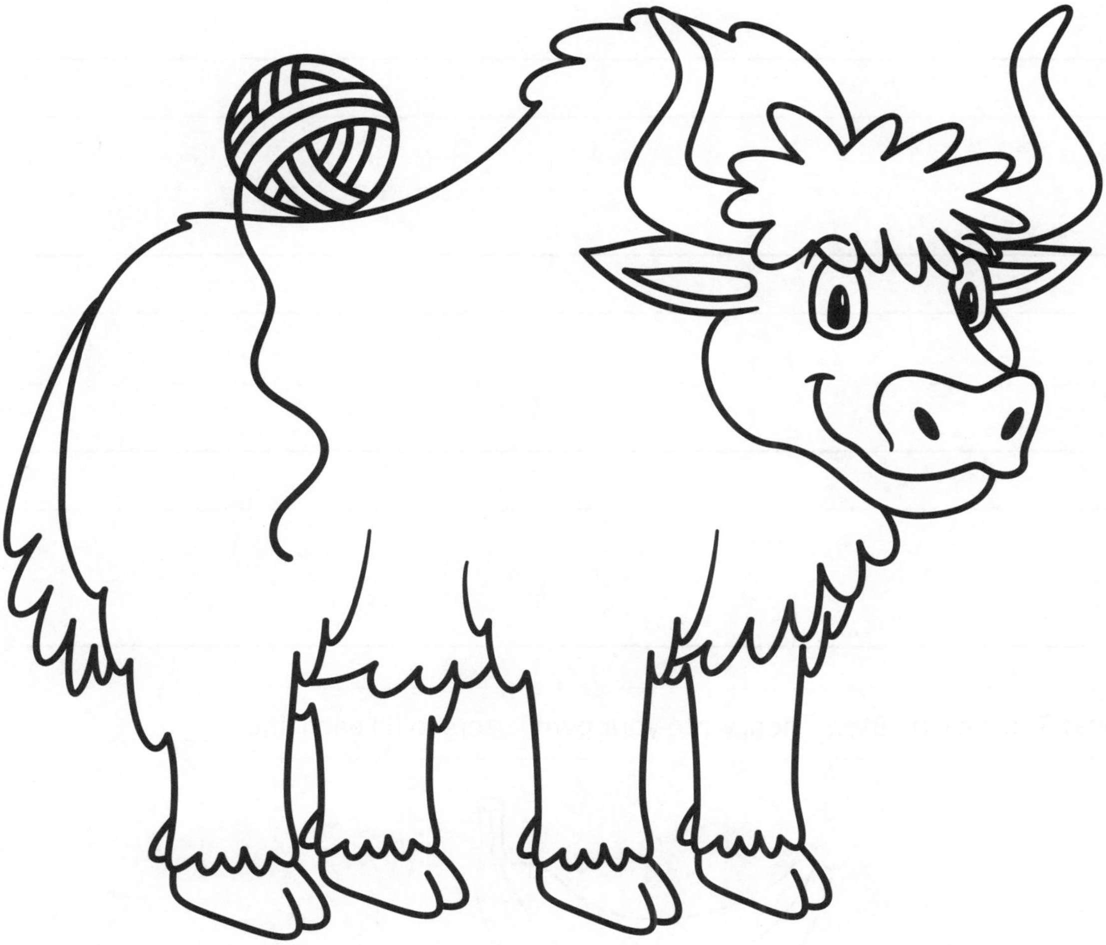

Some yellow

_arn on a _ak.

Directions: Fill in the blanks with a lowercase *y*. Color the yarn yellow. Then, color the yak.

Review

Name: _____

w

W

x

x

Directions: Trace each letter. Then, write your own letters to fill each line.

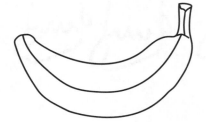

yellow ellow

yes

Directions: Trace each letter. Then, write the missing letter to complete the word. Write the word two more times.

Name: _____

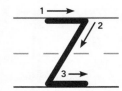 

Directions: Start at the star. Trace each line.

Name: _____

Print Lowercase

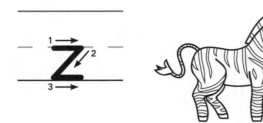

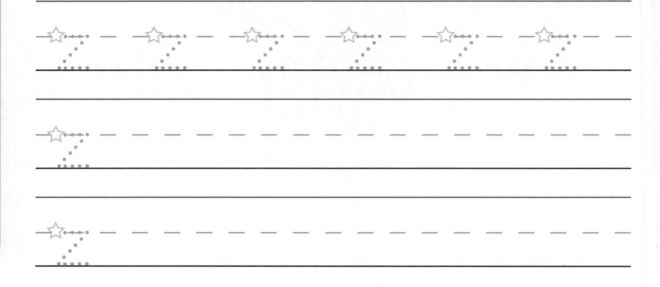

Directions: Start at the star. Trace each letter. Then, write your own letters to fill the lines.

z ebra   ebra

z ipper   ipper

z oo   oo

Directions: Trace the letters. Then, write the missing letter to complete each word.

Name: _____

Z

Directions: Start at the star. Trace each letter. Then, write your own letters to fill the lines.

ach   ach

ora   ora

ane   ane

Directions: Trace the letters. Then, write the missing letter to complete each name.

Name: _____

Activity

Directions: Trace each line. Then, color the picture.

130193—180 Days of Printing: Beginning

Name: _____

Y

Z

Directions: Trace each letter. Then, write your own letters to fill each line.

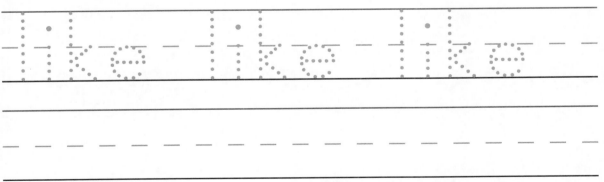

Directions: Trace each word. Then, write the word two more times.

Name: _____

Directionality and Strokes

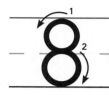

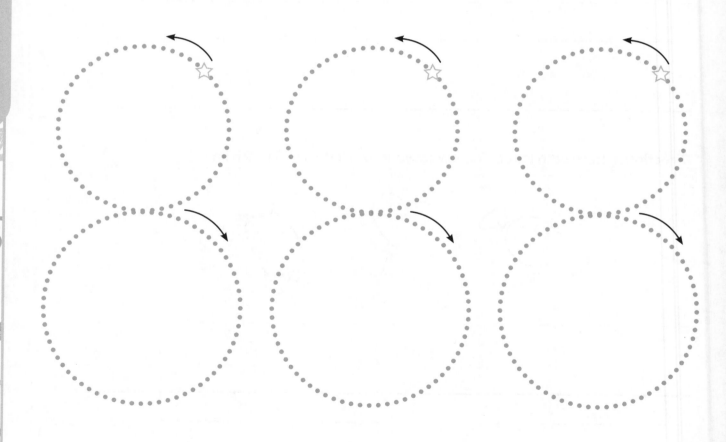

_____

Directions: Start at the star. Connect the dots.

130193—180 Days of Printing: Beginning

Name: _____

8 eight

Directions: Start at the star. Trace each number. Then, write your own numbers on the lines.

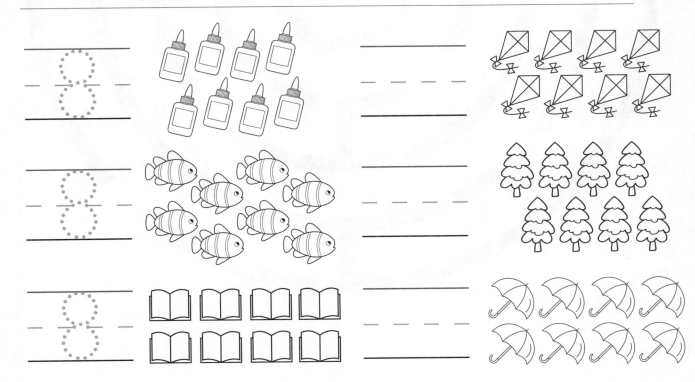

Directions: Count the objects. Trace the numbers. Then, write the numbers.

Print

Name: _____

Start

End

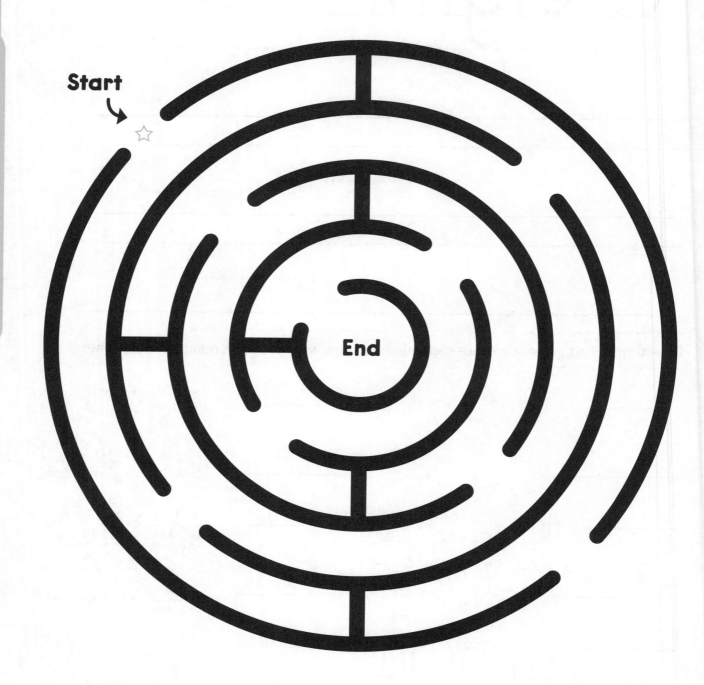

Directions: Complete the maze.

Name: _____

1 ●

2 ●

3 ●

4 ●

5 ●

6 ●

7 ●

8 ●

Directions: Connect the dots. Count as you draw. Then, color the picture.

Review

Name: _____

2

4

6

8

Directions: Trace each number. Then, write your own to fill each line.

There are
flowers.

Directions: Count the flowers. Write the number in the sentence.

130193—180 Days of Printing: Beginning

Name: _____

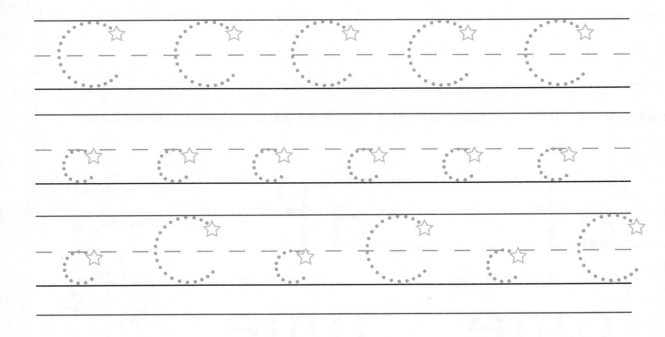

Directions: Start at the star. Connect the dots. Then, copy the pattern.

Name: _____

Print Lowercase

c

c c c c c c

c

c

Directions: Start at the star. Trace each letter. Then, write your own letters to fill the lines.

cat   at

come   ome

car   ar

Directions: Trace the letters. Then, write the missing letter to complete each word.

130193—180 Days of Printing: Beginning   © Shell Education

Name: _____

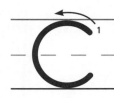 

Print Uppercase

Directions: Start at the star. Trace each letter. Then, write your own letters to fill the lines.

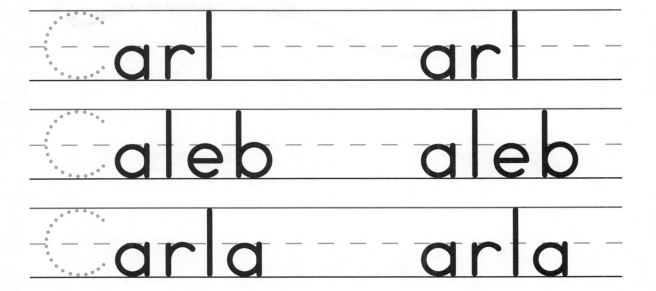

Carl   arl

Caleb   aleb

Carla   arla

Directions: Trace the letters. Then, write the missing letter to complete each name.

Name: _____

Activity

Directions: Connect the dots. Then, color the picture.

130193—180 Days of Printing: Beginning

Name: _____

cat
like
the

Directions: Trace each word. Then, write your own words to fill each line.

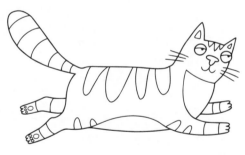

I like cats.
The cat runs.

Directions: Trace each word to finish the sentences.

Directionality and Strokes

Name: _____

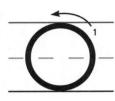 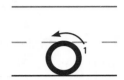

Directions: Start at the star. Trace each circle.

Name: _____

Directions: Start at the star. Trace each letter. Then, write your own letters to fill the lines.

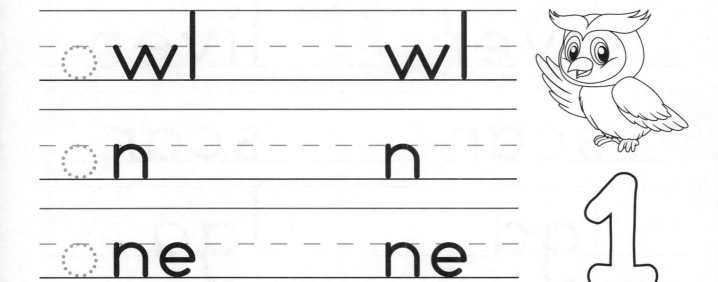

Directions: Trace the letters. Then, write the missing letter to complete each word.

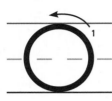

Name: _____

Print Uppercase

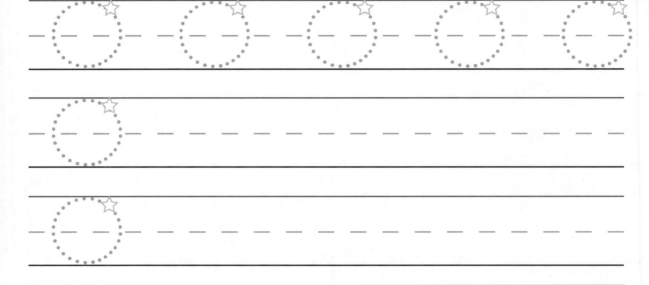

Directions: Start at the star. Trace each letter. Then, write your own letters to fill the lines.

Oliver   liver

Oscar   scar

Olga   lga

Directions: Trace the letters. Then, write the missing letter to complete each name.

Name: _____

Activity

Directions: Trace each circle. Add more bubbles. Then, color the picture.

130193—180 Days of Printing: Beginning

Name:

for

I

look

see

Directions: Trace each word. Then, write your own words to fill each line.

I see you.
You look happy.

Directions: Trace each word to finish the sentences.

Name: _____

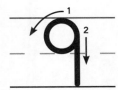

Directions: Start at the star. Connect the dots.

Name: _____

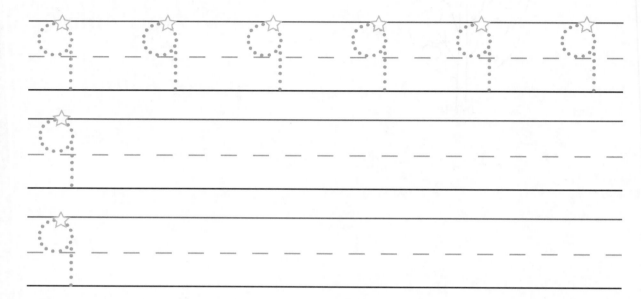

Directions: Start at the star. Trace each number. Then, write your own numbers on the lines.

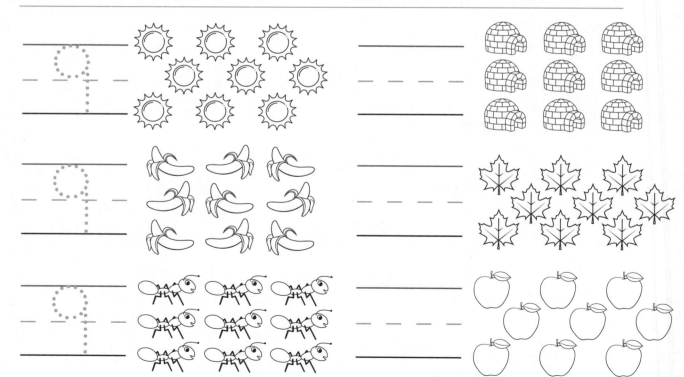

Directions: Count the objects. Trace the numbers. Then, write the numbers.

Directions: Count the stripes. Then, color the stripes in two different colors.

Name: _____

Activity

Directions: Connect the dots. Count the petals. Then, color the picture.

Name: _____

1

3

5

7

9

Directions: Trace each number. Then, write your own to fill each line.

There are ____ kites.

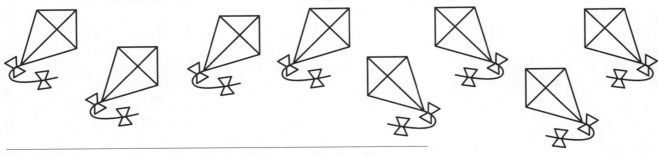

Directions: Count the kites. Write the number in the sentence.

Name: _____

Directionality and Strokes

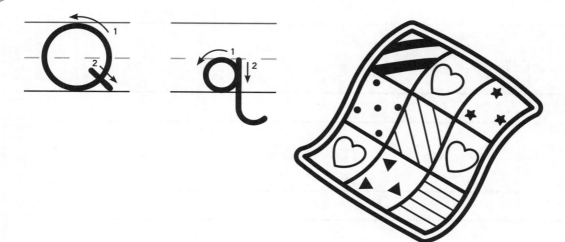

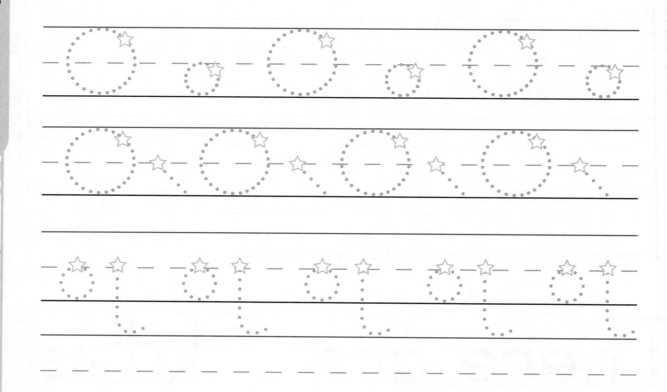

Directions: Start at the star. Connect the dots. Then, write your own pattern.

130193—180 Days of Printing: Beginning

Name: _____

q

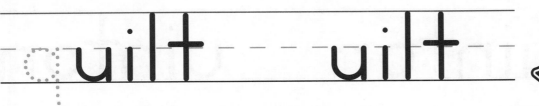

☆ ☆ ☆ ☆ ☆ ☆

☆

☆

Directions: Start at the star. Trace each letter. Then, write your own letters to fill the lines.

uilt   uilt

ueen   ueen

uick   uick

Directions: Trace the letters. Then, write the missing letter to complete each word.

© Shell Education   130193—180 Days of Printing: Beginning

Name: _____

Print Uppercase

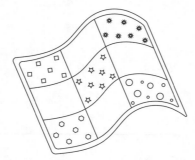

Q · · Q · · Q · · Q · · Q

Q · · · · · · · · · · · · ·

Q · · · · · · · · · · · · ·

Directions: Start at the star. Trace each letter. Then, write your own letters to fill the lines.

Quinton   uinton

Quil   uil

Quincy   uincy

Directions: Trace the letters. Then, write the missing letter to complete each name.

Name: _____

Directions: Color the shapes with uppercase *Q* yellow. Color the shapes with lowercase *q* blue.

© Shell Education

130193—180 Days of Printing: Beginning

Name: _____

Review

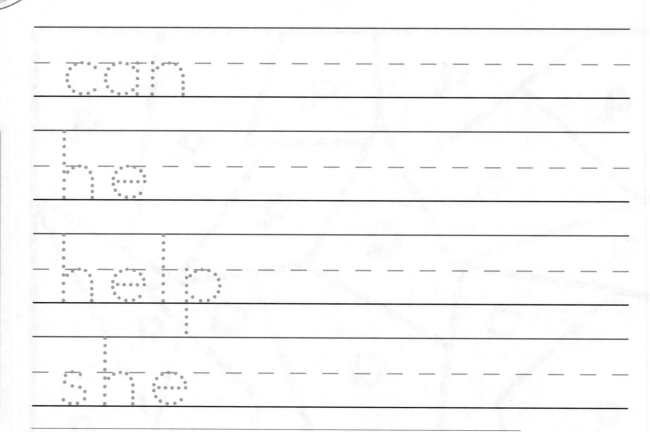

can

he

help

she

Directions: Trace each word. Then, write your own words to fill each line.

He can jump.

She can run.

Directions: Trace each word to finish the sentences.

Name: _____

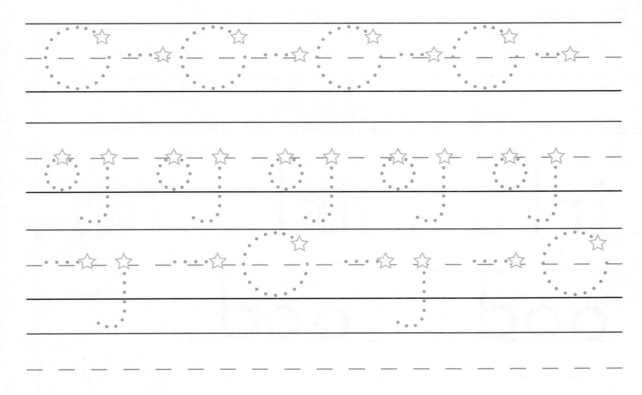

Directions: Start at the star. Connect the dots. Then, write your own pattern.

Name: _____

Print Lowercase

g

g g g g g g

g

g

Directions: Start at the star. Trace each letter. Then, write your own letters to fill the lines.

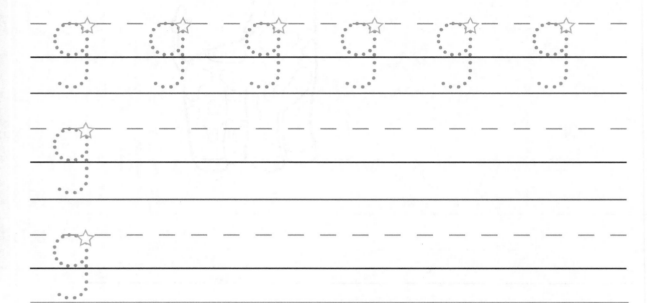

girl   irl

good   ood

pig   pi

Directions: Trace the letters. Then, write the missing letter to complete each word.

Name: _____

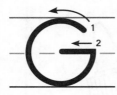

Print Uppercase

Directions: Start at the star. Trace each letter. Then, write your own letters to fill the lines.

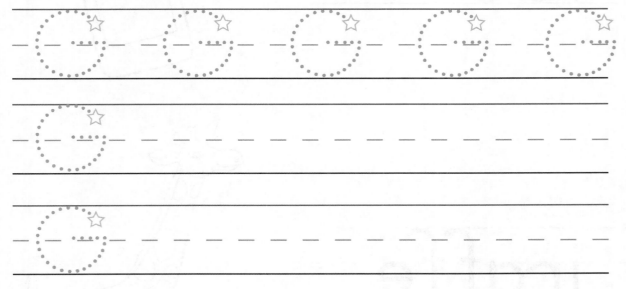

George   eorge

Gab   ab

Grant   rant

Directions: Trace the letters. Then, write the missing letter to complete each name.

Name: _____

Activity

lue

iraffe

oat

Directions: Write a *g* to complete each word. Then, color the pictures.

130193—180 Days of Printing: Beginning

Name: _____

find

go

good

now

Directions: Trace each word. Then, write your own words to fill each line.

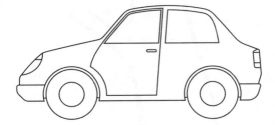

The car can go

Good job!

Directions: Trace each word to finish the sentences.

Review

Name: _____

Directionality and Strokes

Directions: Circle the numbers. Then, color the tree.

Name: _____

$\overset{\curvearrowleft}{O}_1$ zero

O O O O O O

O

O

10   15

11   16

12   17

13   18

14   19

Directions: Start at the star. Trace each number. Then, write your own numbers on the lines.

Name: _____

Activity

Directions: Trace the numbers.

130193—180 Days of Printing: Beginning

© Shell Education

1

2

3

_____

_____

5

_____

_____

7

8

_____

10

_____

_____

12

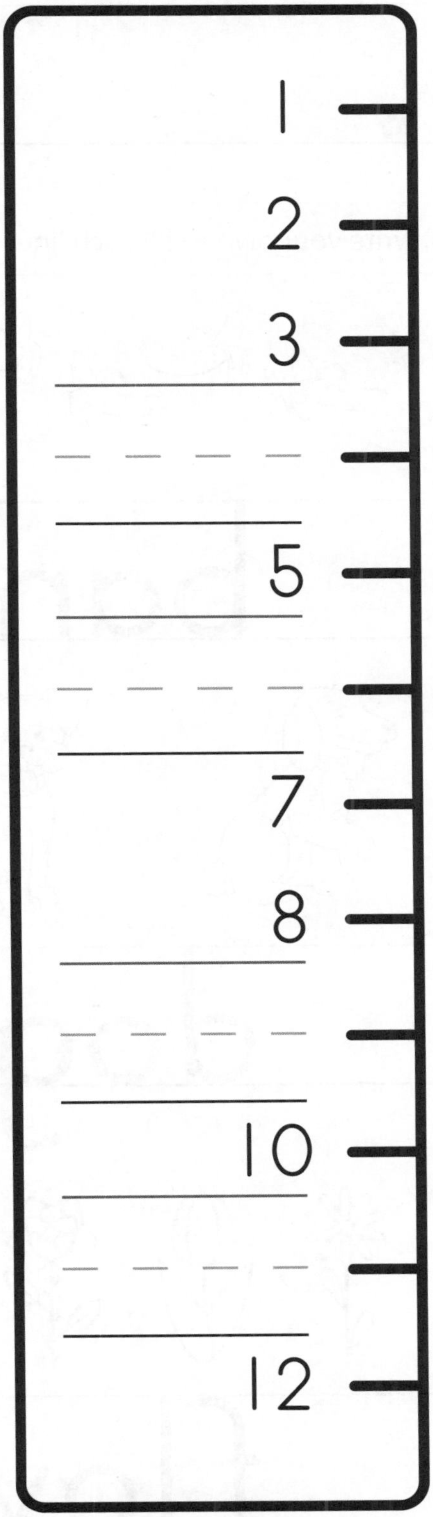

Directions: Write the missing numbers.

Name: _____

Review

10

Directions: Trace each number. Then, write your own to fill each line.

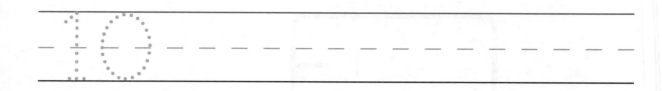

I see _____ bananas.

I see _____ dogs.

I see _____ flowers.

Directions: Count the objects. Write the numbers in the sentences.

Name: _____

S̆ s̆

Directions: Start at the star. Trace each curve. Then, write your own line.

130193—180 Days of Printing: Beginning

Name: _____

Print Lowercase

s̄

☆s ☆s ☆s ☆s ☆s ☆s ☆s

☆s

☆s

Directions: Start at the star. Trace each letter. Then, write your own letters to fill the lines.

un   un

ee   ee

pleae pleae

Directions: Trace the letters. Then, write the missing letter to complete each word.

Name: _____

S

S S S S S S

S

S

Directions: Start at the star. Trace each letter. Then, write your own letters to fill the lines.

Sam   am

Simone   imone

Sophia   ophia

Directions: Trace the letters. Then, write the missing letter to complete each name.

Name: _____

Activity

Directions: Trace each curve. Practice writing a curved letter without picking up your pencil. Then, color the pictures.

Name: _____

said

see

there

yes

Directions: Trace each word. Then, write your own words to fill each line.

I see a dog.

Directions: Trace the sentence. Then, write the sentence on the line.

Review

Name: _____

Directionality and Strokes

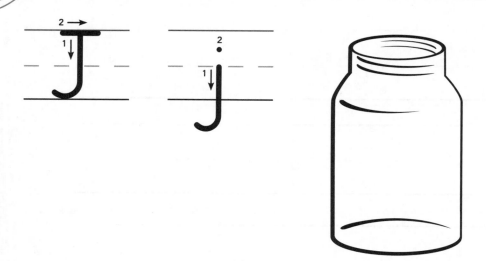

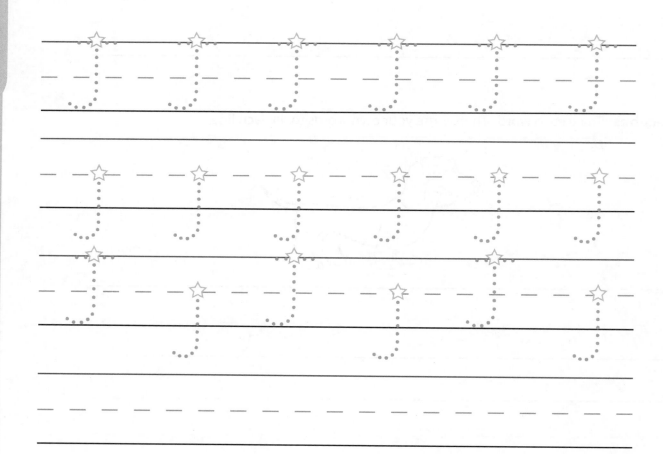

Directions: Start at the star. Connect the dots. Then, write your own pattern.

Name: _____

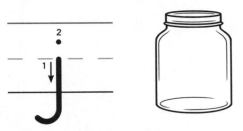

j

Directions: Start at the star. Trace each letter. Then, write your own letters to fill the lines.

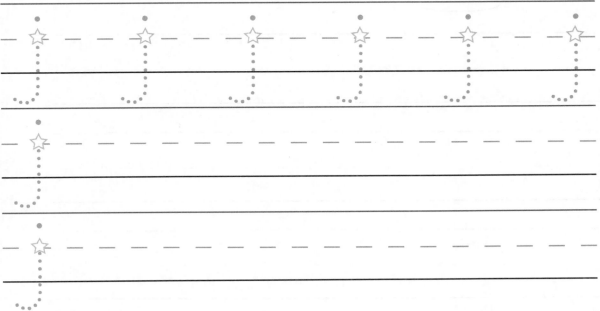

ar ar

ump ump

acket acket

Directions: Trace the letters. Then, write the missing letter to complete each word.

Print Uppercase

Name: _____

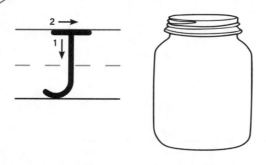

Directions: Start at the star. Trace each letter. Then, write your own letters to fill the lines.

Jessica   Jessica

Jay   Jay

Jerome   Jerome

Directions: Trace the letters. Then, write the missing letter to complete each name.

Name: _____

Jill with a jar.

Activity

Directions: Color the uppercase *J* and lowercase *j*. Then, color the picture.

Name: _____

Review

eat

I

like

to

Directions: Trace the words. Then, write your own words to fill each line.

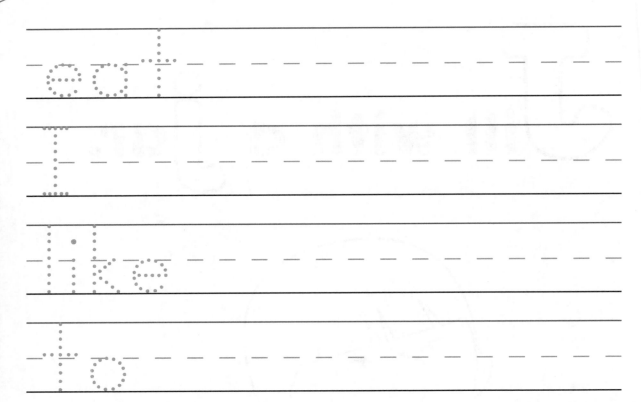

I like to eat.

Directions: Trace the sentence. Then, write the sentence on the line.

Lowercase Letter Guide

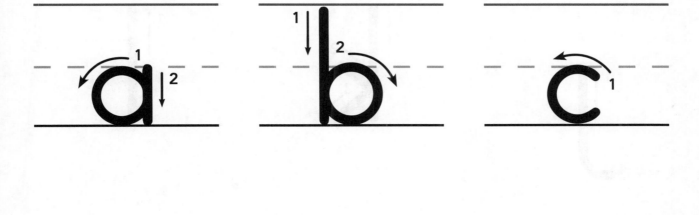

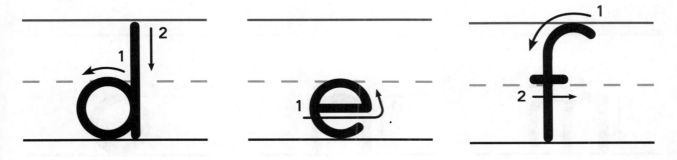

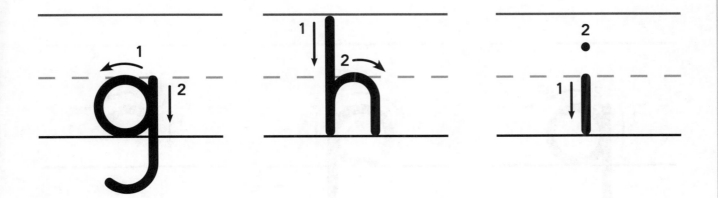

Directions: Practice making each lowercase letter. Trace each letter with your finger, make it from modeling clay, or use objects to make the letter.

Lowercase Letter Guide *(cont.)*

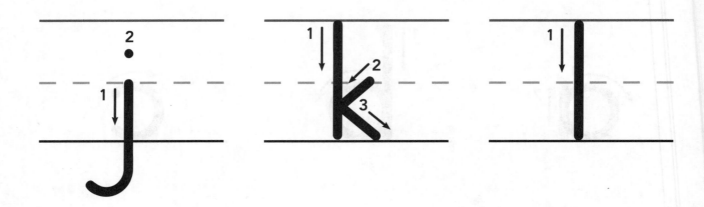

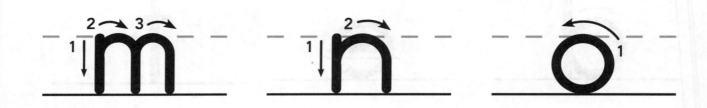

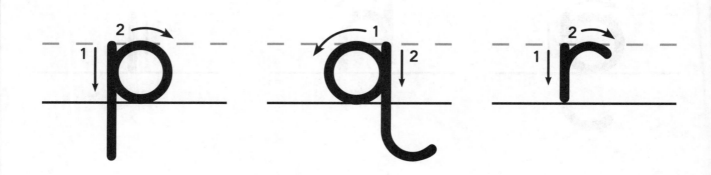

Lowercase Letter Guide *(cont.)*

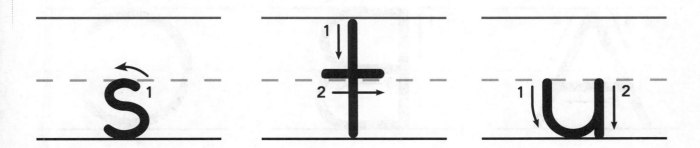

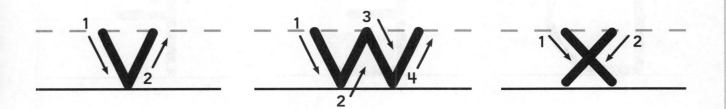

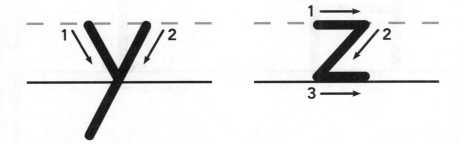

Uppercase Letter Guide

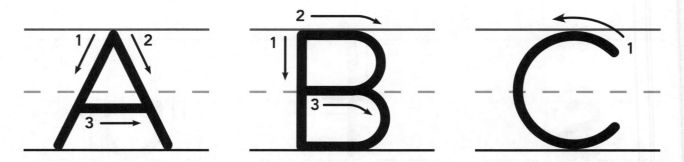

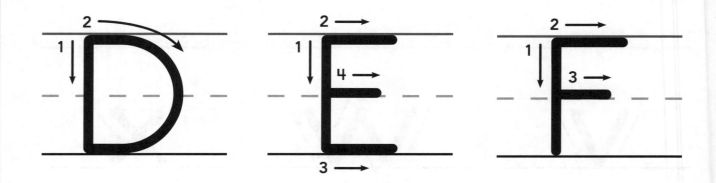

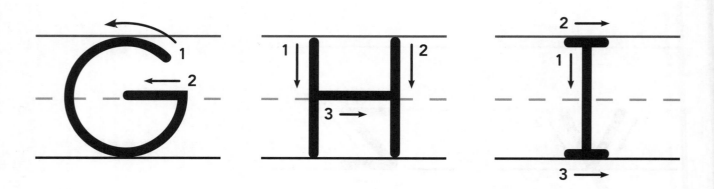

Directions: Practice making each uppercase letter. Trace each letter with your finger, make it from modeling clay, or use objects to make the letter.

Uppercase Letter Guide (cont.)

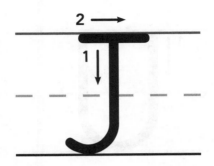 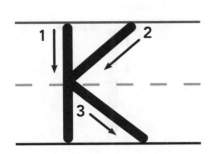 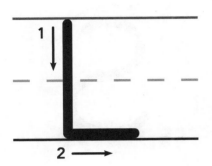

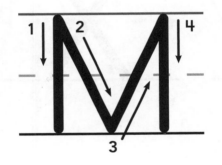 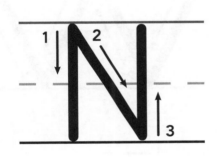 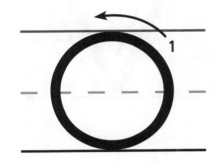

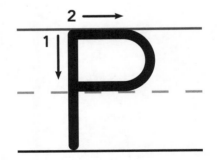 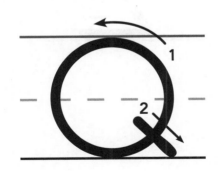 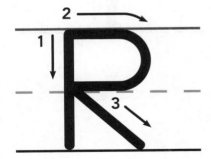

Uppercase Letter Guide *(cont.)*

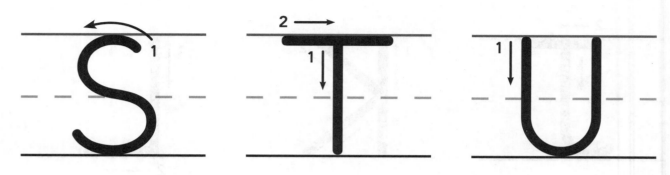

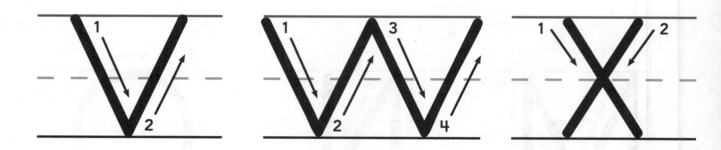

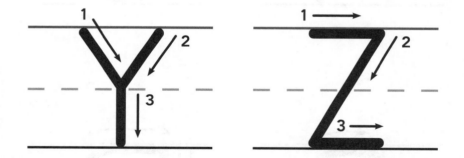

Number Guide

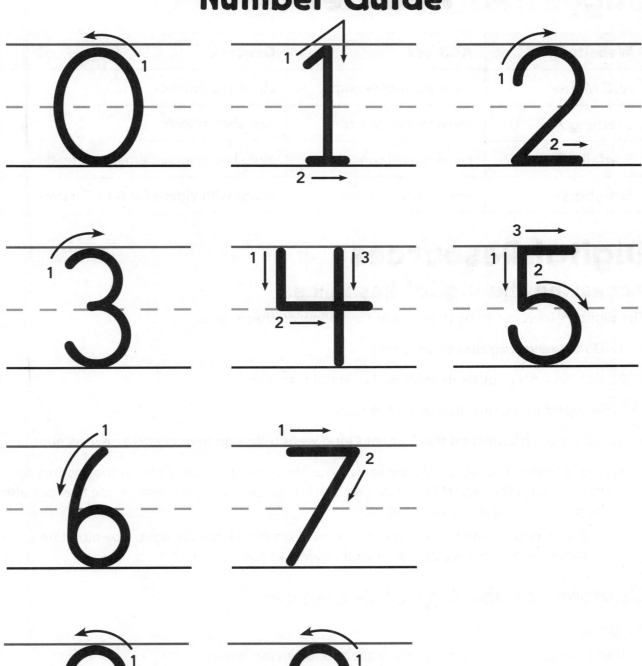

Directions: Practice making each number. Trace each number with your finger, make it from modeling clay, or use objects to make the number.

Suggested Websites

Website Title	Address	Content
ABC Mouse	www.abcmouse.com	alphabet, phonics
Learning A–Z	www.learninga-z.com	alphabet, phonics
Starfall	www.starfall.com	alphabet, phonics, emergent reading
Storybots	www.storybots.com	songs with videos for A-to-Z letters

Digital Resources

Accessing the Digital Resources

The digital resources can be downloaded by following these steps:

1. Go to **www.tcmpub.com/digital**

2. Use the ISBN number to redeem the digital resources.

3. Respond to the question using the book.

4. Follow the prompts on the Content Cloud website to sign in or create a new account.

5. The redeemed content will now be on your My Content screen. Click on the product to look through the Digital Resources. All files can be downloaded, while some files can also be previewed, opened, and shared.

   • Please note: Some files provided for download have large file sizes. Download times for these larger files vary based on your download speed.

Contents of the Digital Resources

Activities

• Hands-on practice for writing uppercase and lowercase letters
• Sentence-writing practice
• Handwriting lines for printing activities